CARAVANNING THROUGH FRANCE

By the same author

**Caravanning through Belgium,
Holland and Luxembourg**

CARAVANNING THROUGH FRANCE

Harry Phillips

CASSELL · LONDON

CASSELL & COMPANY LTD

an imprint of
Cassell & Collier Macmillan Publishers Ltd
35 Red Lion Square, London WC1R 4SG
and at Sydney, Auckland, Toronto, Johannesburg

and an affiliate of The Macmillan Publishing Company Inc, New York

First published 1975

ISBN 0 304 29422 5

Filmset and printed by BAS Printers Limited, Wallop, Hampshire
F 175

INTRODUCTION

Pauline Hallam
Director of Public Relations
French Government Tourist Office

I am pleased to have the opportunity to write the introduction to Harry Phillips's new book because it describes the wonderful opportunities for caravanners in France; in welcoming our British caravanning friends through the medium of this book I can recommend that it will be of value to all caravanners of whatever nationality.

The new legislation designed to improve 'le camping' facilities illustrates the keen interest shown in caravanning by the French Government and, in the short time since its introduction, this legislation has had the effect of further improving already high standards.

There is a comprehensive selection of well-organized sites throughout the country and the joys of caravanning in France are being appreciated by greater numbers every year. Caravanning answers the deep longing to move about felt by more and more people and France caters for every taste, offers every kind of scenery, every variety of holiday attraction.

Few countries can boast of such a fine, well-planned network of roads totalling 700,000 kilometres, seventeen times the earth's circumference. Caravanners will enjoy the changing scenery, tall poplars lining the roads of the Île-de-France, oak trees shading roads of the Périgord, plane trees spreading over those of Provence; roads leading to mountains, to rivers, lakes, seas and beaches, castles, museums, cathedrals and many exciting sites of natural beauty.

France offers a warm welcome to all caravanners.

To Emma and Huncamunca

CONTENTS

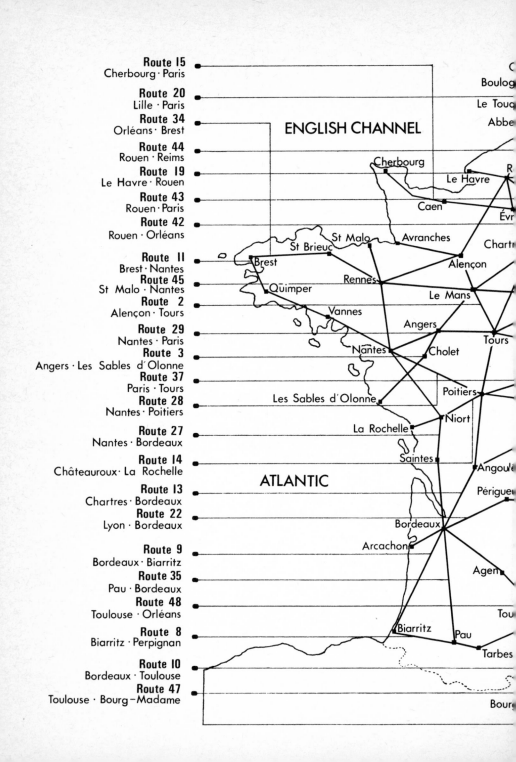

Route 15
Cherbourg · Paris

Route 20
Lille · Paris

Route 34
Orléans · Brest

Route 44
Rouen · Reims

Route 19
Le Havre · Rouen

Route 43
Rouen · Paris

Route 42
Rouen · Orléans

Route 11
Brest · Nantes

Route 45
St Malo · Nantes

Route 2
Alençon · Tours

Route 29
Nantes · Paris

Route 3
Angers · Les Sables d'Olonne

Route 37
Paris · Tours

Route 28
Nantes · Poitiers

Route 27
Nantes · Bordeaux

Route 14
Châteauroux · La Rochelle

Route 13
Chartres · Bordeaux

Route 22
Lyon · Bordeaux

Route 9
Bordeaux · Biarritz

Route 35
Pau · Bordeaux

Route 48
Toulouse · Orléans

Route 8
Biarritz · Perpignan

Route 10
Bordeaux · Toulouse

Route 47
Toulouse · Bourg—Madame

ENGLISH CHANNEL

Cherbourg

Le Havre

Caen

Évr

St Malo

Avranches

Chartr

St Brieuc

Alençon

Brest

Rennes

Le Mans

Quimper

Le Mans

Vannes

Angers

Tours

Nantes

Cholet

Poitiers

Les Sables d'Olonne

Niort

La Rochelle

Saintes

Angoulê

ATLANTIC

Périgueu

Bordeaux

Arcachon

Agen

Tou

Biarritz

Pau

Tarbes

Bour

Boulog

Le Touq

Abbe

R

Boug

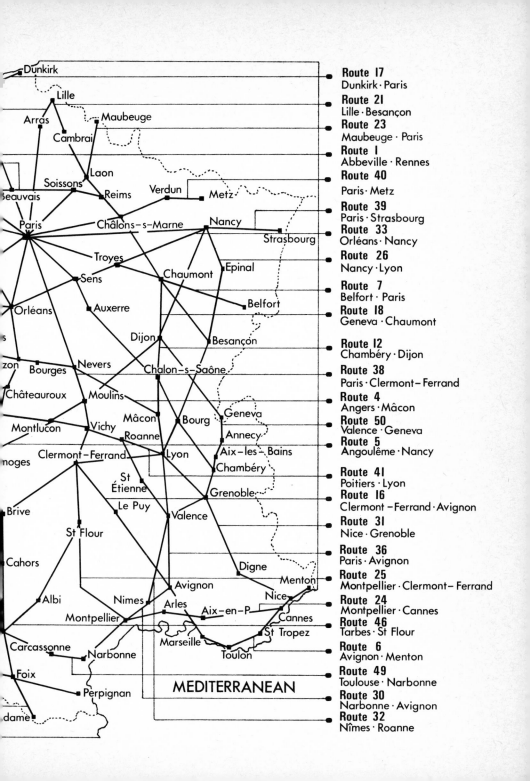

Dunkirk

Lille

Arras

Maubeuge

Cambrai

Beauvais

Laon

Soissons

Reims

Verdun

Metz

Paris

Châlons–s–Marne

Nancy

Strasbourg

Troyes

Epinal

Sens

Chaumont

Orléans

Auxerre

Belfort

Dijon

Besançon

Nevers

Chalon–s–Saône

Bourges

Châteauroux

Moulins

Mâcon

Bourg

Geneva

Montluçon

Vichy

Roanne

Annecy

Clermont–Ferrand

Lyon

Aix–les–Bains

Limoges

St Étienne

Chambéry

Le Puy

Grenoble

Brive

Valence

St Flour

Cahors

Digne

Menton

Avignon

Nice

Albi

Nimes

Arles

Aix–en–P

Cannes

Montlucon

Montpellier

St Tropez

Carcassonne

Marseille

Toulon

Narbonne

Foix

MEDITERRANEAN

Perpignan

N. Dame

Route 17
Dunkirk · Paris

Route 21
Lille · Besançon

Route 23
Maubeuge · Paris

Route 1
Abbeville · Rennes

Route 40
Paris · Metz

Route 39
Paris · Strasbourg

Route 33
Orléans · Nancy

Route 26
Nancy · Lyon

Route 7
Belfort · Paris

Route 18
Geneva · Chaumont

Route 12
Chambéry · Dijon

Route 38
Paris · Clermont–Ferrand

Route 4
Angers · Mâcon

Route 50
Valence · Geneva

Route 5
Angoulême · Nancy

Route 41
Poitiers · Lyon

Route 16
Clermont–Ferrand · Avignon

Route 31
Nice · Grenoble

Route 36
Paris · Avignon

Route 25
Montpellier · Clermont–Ferrand

Route 24
Montpellier · Cannes

Route 46
Tarbes · St Flour

Route 6
Avignon · Menton

Route 49
Toulouse · Narbonne

Route 30
Narbonne · Avignon

Route 32
Nîmes · Roanne

ACKNOWLEDGEMENTS

I am indebted to many Departments of the French Government for the facts and figures which they have kindly made available to me; to the many offices of the Syndicat d'Initiative who have patiently dealt with my considerable demands upon their time; and particularly to Pauline Hallam, Director of Public Relations, French Government Tourist Office, London.

For the photographs in support of my own I have pleasure in acknowledging the French Government Tourist Office.

The route-map and illustrated maps are by Anthony Hall and Linda Wheeler, Smile Design, Gosport, Hampshire.

Part I

THE MAGIC OF 'LE CAMPING'

1 SUMMARY OF ROUTE DETAILS

(Author's Own Route Numbers)

Route 1   ABBEVILLE to RENNES, via Dieppe, Rouen (Avranches)

Route 2   ALENÇON to TOURS

Route 3   ANGERS to LES SABLES D'OLONNE via Cholet

Route 4   ANGERS to MÂCON via Tours, Vierzon, Bourges, Nevers

Route 5   ANGOULÊME to NANCY via Montluçon, Moulins, Dijon

Route 6   AVIGNON to MENTON via Marseille, Toulon, St. Tropez, Cannes, Nice, Monte Carlo

Route 7   BELFORT to PARIS via Chaumont, Troyes

Route 8   BIARRITZ to PERPIGNAN via Pau, Tarbes, Foix

Route 9   BORDEAUX to BIARRITZ

Route 10   BORDEAUX to TOULOUSE via Agen

Route 11   BREST to NANTES via Quimper, Vannes

Route 12   CHAMBÉRY to DIJON via Bourg, Chalon-sur-Saône

Route 13   CHARTRES to BORDEAUX via Tours, Poitiers, Angoulême

Route 14   CHÂTEAUROUX to LA ROCHELLE via Poitiers, Niort

Route 15   CHERBOURG to PARIS via Caen, Evreux

Route 16   CLERMONT-FERRAND to AVIGNON via Le Puy

Route 17   DUNKIRK to PARIS via Calais, Boulogne, Abbeville, Beauvais

Route 18   GENEVA (Switzerland) to CHAUMONT via Dijon

Route 19   LE HAVRE to ROUEN

Route 20   LILLE to PARIS via Arras

Route 21 LILLE to BESANÇON via Cambrai, Laon, Reims, Châlons-sur-Marne, Chaumont

Route 22 LYON to BORDEAUX via Clermont-Ferrand, Brive, Périgueux

Route 23 MAUBEUGE to PARIS via Laon, Soissons

Route 24 MONTPELLIER to CANNES via Arles, Aix-en-Provence

Route 25 MONTPELLIER to CLERMONT-FERRAND via Millau, St. Flour

Route 26 NANCY to LYON via Epinal, Besançon, Bourg

Route 27 NANTES to BORDEAUX via Niort

Route 28 NANTES to POITIERS

Route 29 NANTES to PARIS via Angers, Le Mans, Chartres

Route 30 NARBONNE to AVIGNON via Montpellier, Nîmes

Route 31 NICE to GRENOBLE via Digne

Route 32 NÎMES to ROANNE via Valence, St. Étienne

Route 33 ORLÉANS to NANCY via Sens, Troyes

Route 34 ORLÉANS to BREST via Le Mans, Rennes, St. Brieuc

Route 35 PAU to BORDEAUX

Route 36 PARIS to AVIGNON via Auxerre, Chalon-sur-Saône, Mâcon, Lyon, Valence

Route 37 PARIS to TOURS via Orléans, Blois

Route 38 PARIS to CLERMONT-FERRAND via Nevers, Moulins, Vichy

Route 39 PARIS to STRASBOURG via Nancy

Route 40 PARIS to METZ via Châlons-sur-Marne, Verdun

Route 41 POITIERS to LYON via Montluçon, Roanne

Route 42 ROUEN to ORLÉANS via Evreux, Chartres

Route 43 ROUEN to PARIS

Route 44 ROUEN to REIMS via Beauvais, Soissons

Route 45 ST. MALO to NANTES via Rennes

Route 46 TARBES to ST.-FLOUR via Toulouse, Albi

Route 47 TOULOUSE to BOURG-MADAME via Foix

Route 48 TOULOUSE to ORLÉANS via Cahors, Brive, Limoges, Châteauroux, Vierzon

Route 49 TOULOUSE to NARBONNE via Carcassonne

Route 50 VALENCE to GENEVA (Switzerland) via Chambéry, Aix-les-Bains, Annecy

2 CARAVAN LIFE IN FRANCE

A caravan is a magic carpet and for the caravanner who is eager to make the most of his mobility, France is the most magic country to explore.

Caravanning character varies from country to country and France is one of the best, certainly one of the best in which to make a start. The attitude towards 'le camping' is generous, hospitable and understanding; the sites are widespread, mostly with excellent facilities and well disciplined, often landscaped (whether intentionally or not); rarely in France do you come across acres of caravans in vast lines from hedge to hedge, as monotonous as a display of shoe-boxes. If you have any prejudice against large, organized sites you can forget it in France.

The majority of caravanners and campers use regular sites, but you can caravan and camp in solitary fashion in the wild, subject to certain conditions, the most important being that you must obtain permission from the landowner – one of the few occasions on a French caravan holiday when a knowledge of the language is necessary.

You are not permitted to caravan or camp by public roads nor on public beaches.

Farm camping and forest camping is growing every year, but the security of an approved and guarded site is preferred by most caravanners. No camping or caravanning outside authorized sites is allowed in the south of France because of the danger of fire.

Caravans, motor-caravans, trailer-tents and tents are not segregated on French sites, except on a few specialized sites, and all are welcome. Mostly you are free to choose your own pitch on a site without restriction except the obvious one of reserving electrically wired pitches, which are usually in groups or rows, for those who can use them.

The tent or trailer-tent is not the poor relation of the caravan in France where the enjoyment of 'le camping' is happily universal. In England, as you know, we segregate ourselves, caravans curling superior towbars at tents who flap their exclusiveness in reply. We have allowed The Planners to create this situation in England presumably because we want it this way. But I much prefer the freedom of 'le camping', the joining together in a common purpose, everybody, all classes, a king in his tent or a cat in his caravan.

If you have never caravanned you may be assured that towing presents no difficulty to the average car driver; if you have never caravanned in France you may be glad to know that the facilities there will almost certainly be better than any you have so far encountered.

If you drive a car it is never too early nor too late to take to the road with a caravan or motor-caravan, not as a compromise because hotel touring is impossibly expensive, but as a pleasure in its own right. Hotel touring means living out of a suitcase, wondering what each new bedroom will be like; your caravan is your foreign bedroom whose wardrobe you fill outside your home front door. Hotel mealtimes and menus are theirs, whilst caravan meals and times are all within your choice and control. And finding a good site is a great deal easier than finding a satisfactory hotel.

If you are able to choose it is preferable to take your caravan holiday in France outside the peak tourist month of August, the ideal time being May or June. Early on you have lay-bys to yourself, although a number of sites may not be open. The avoidance of August does not apply only to caravan holidays, of course; it is well known that all France is on holiday from about the middle of July until the end of August, at which time all leisure facilities are overcrowded.

Certain areas are more popular than others, but this popularity creates caravan sites equal to the demand except in the peak holiday period. Obviously certain times are more popular than others: weekends, for instance, and public holidays. You should be safely snugged in at a pleasant site before any rush starts.

This book sets out to be a guide to caravanning in France, a guide to the character of the different regions and to some of the country's various tourist attractions, with a countrywide selection of camping sites nearby. It does not attempt to take the place of the annual guides that provide the changing data of opening dates and site charges plus a comprehensive list of camping sites in France. This book shows nearly six hundred sites in the Routes Section and directs you to areas where camping sites are plentiful. You will by now have gathered that when you talk about a camping site in France you mean a caravan site and vice versa. Where no site is shown against the name of a town in the Routes Section you can take it that there is no site there. The approximate number of camping sites in each province is shown in the Provinces Section. If you are happy to take pot luck, as we are, you will simply pull in at a camping site in the place where you happen to be. Only very occasionally will you find yourself pulling into static or residential sites where each pitch has been bought as a permanent holiday home by a caravan owner. However, if you know an owner and he is away from the site, he may give you permission to use his pitch in his absence. Otherwise, static sites are of no interest to the touring caravanner.

In the really popular areas it is likely that you will take pot luck anyhow. 'Camping' signs are now displayed in the majority of French towns and villages that possess a site.

The principal annual guides to caravanning in France are:

Michelin Camping Caravanning en France. Selected sites are listed alphabetically,

You have lay-bys to yourself

with opening dates and charges. Although written in French there are explanatory notes and explanations of symbols in English. The Michelin Guide is published in April/May, is available at bookshops in England.

If you become a member of the Touring Club de France (178 Piccadilly, London, W1V 0AL), for your annual subscription with extra for the Plein Air-Camping Section you will receive the Indicateur du Camping Caravanning, an alphabetical list of French camping sites with opening dates and charges, published annually. You will also be entitled to use, and to receive priority over non-T.C.F. members at, the thirty or so Camps Privés du T.C.F. Some camping sites in France advertise discounts to T.C.F. members, but in my experience they are not always offered.

Guide Susse (12 francs), lists French sites with opening dates and charges but is grouped in départements; this is not always so easy to follow when touring but in this book, in the Routes Section, every département is shown as the routes pass through them. An index in the Guide Susse lists every site alphabetically. Guide Susse is written in French but there are explanatory notes in English.

The *A.A. Camping and Caravanning Overseas Guide* covers thirty-nine countries from Afghanistan to Yugoslavia. About a quarter of the sites in France are listed alphabetically, with opening dates and charges. There is a useful map showing the situation of sites; in fact it is the only map, I think, that unfolds to show the whole of the country, which is very helpful when planning your holiday.

There are other guides covering France and many other countries as well.

Dates of opening of camping sites may change from year to year and even the dates given in the above-named guides do not always agree. But you can take it that where a site is shown to be open *permanently* this information is more likely to be correct than the dates of seasonal openings. In this book the names of permanently open sites are printed in capital letters.

Sites that are recommended to you do not always turn out as recommended. This is not to say that the recommendation is not given in good faith; but what suits me may not suit you. There are so many personal factors involved. Camping site comparison is a favourite topic of conversation amongst fellow nationals caravanning abroad and my wife and I never cease to be amazed at the adverse comments made about sites that we considered excellent and vice versa.

We have wasted hours searching for recommended sites – at one time, once a site had been recommended to us we developed a fixation about finding it – only to discover that the site was no more special (to us) than many we had passed. Once a site is recommended it seems to hide away, to place itself at an inconvenient distance from your intended route. To all the caravanners who have recommended sites to us I offer my apologies; we will go there one day, one day we will be passing that way.

This is the key to site-seeking. Make up your mind what part of the country you wish to explore and drive in that direction in the expectation that there will always be a camping site available.

If you are new to towing a caravan I must admit that the initial restraint upon the performance of your car will be disconcerting. The car will seem to take an age to climb up into higher gears. You will be anxiously studying the distance between you and the vehicle ahead and the distance from other obstructions. Suddenly, after only a hundred miles or so, the caravan behind will be almost forgotten and you will be judging the pace of your car, the gears and the extra width without any conscious effort.

You soon get accustomed to seeing in the rear view mirror what appears to be a warehouse following you, and you will instinctively transfer your attention to the wing mirrors instead (unless, of course, you have equipped your car with a central periscope mirror).

The reduced response to the accelerator that at first makes you feel as though you were driving through treacle is overcome by a more lively use of the gears to urge your outfit up to a speed at which you are nicely 'rolling' along.

Surprisingly enough this restraint is a discipline and a revelation. The joy of relaxed driving at a lower speed than usual is a discovery that the majority of motorists would appreciate. Even when the car is driven without the caravan and seems to spring free, eager to fly like a bird, this restraint is still upon the driver, not as the safety discipline it should be but as pure enjoyment. We all drive too fast and caravan towing is an eye-opening discipline. Having said this, I am assuming that you will, of course, keep in mind the Caravan Code in regard to inconveniencing other road users; watch your rear mirror for traffic that may be balked behind you and pull off the road from time to time if accumulated faster traffic cannot otherwise get past you safely.

A rather special-sounding selection of camping sites in France is the Castels et Camping-Caravaning chain. This was founded in 1959 by the owners of historic houses to provide income to help their estates to survive. The situations are picturesque and camp facilities are sometimes provided in the outbuildings of a castle.

When you book in it is likely that the man in the Site Office or Reception will be the owner himself. You will need a Camping Carnet; more about that later.

It is an attractive idea to pitch your caravan in the grounds of an historic château and the owners are making efforts to improve conditions. I have included about a third of them (there are thirty or so), in the Routes Section so that you may come across one in your travels.

But the important thing, first of all, is to make up your mind where you want to go. A first rule of the touring caravanner should be to go somewhere new, to savour a new experience. The *Routes Section* in the second half of the book describes routes that I have devised to cover the whole of France. The Route numbers are my own; the Routes may be explored in any order or you may plan to connect one Route with another. Connections with other Routes are shown.

Wonderful tourist attractions . . . Aigues-Mortes

What other type of holiday is there where you would – not could, but would – see, say, the Bayeux Tapestry, Mont-St.-Michel, the Martell cellars at Cognac, the Châteaux of the Loire, the surfing beaches of the Atlantic coast, a procession at Lourdes? Holidaymakers *could* tour from hotel to hotel to see these attractions, but seldom do; your caravan, your own hotel room on wheels, is truly your magic carpet. Not only do you have the excitement of travelling easily to such wonderful tourist attractions, but the camping sites themselves are a delight, a never-ending source of anticipation and pleasure, for few French sites wholly disappoint.

3 SUITABLE CARAVANS

You want the smallest caravan when you are towing or paying your car-ferry charges and the largest caravan when you stop. Perhaps, one day, someone will design an expanding caravan on the lines of the expanding toilet compartments. Then it will be possible to stop and unhitch, but before winding down the legs, wind out the caravan from ten to twenty feet.

Until then we shall compromise as we do now. There is no doubt that you should choose the smallest caravan in which you can manage to live rather than the largest caravan that you can manage to tow. The accommodation discomfort of a small caravan can be got around with a tent annexe, but the driving discomfort of a too-large caravan can never be overcome.

Your choice obviously depends upon many factors, principally the size of your family and the size and power of your car.

You should be guided by the caravan maker's recommendations on weight limits if the combination of car and caravan is to be completely manageable and safe. The usual formula for a safe combination is that the unloaded caravan should not exceed three-quarters of the car's kerb weight (empty car with full tank). This is for normal touring and the caravan must not be overloaded, certainly not to the point where it is heavier than the loaded car. The various caravan weights are in the maker's catalogue. If you subtract the ex-works weight from the maximum gross weight the answer will be the safe weight to load into the van. The nose-weight is reckoned to be about a tenth of the gross caravan weight for an average size caravan. If you are interested in finding out the exact figures for your caravan, you probably know that you can take it to a weighbridge; when you have weighed the caravan push the wheels off leaving the tow-bar overhanging. Place a block of wood under the tow-bar at coupling height to find out the nose-weight. A family of four on holiday may well need 3 to 4 cwt. of luggage.

Do not judge the performance of your outfit by trials on level roads for in these circumstances you could tow quite a large van with a Mini. If you plan to drive up into the Alps or the Pyrénées the weight ratio should favour the car by a hundredweight or so over the formula; in fact, if you are thinking of towing around mountain passes the caravan weight should not exceed half the weight of the car. Alpine routes should not be tackled with your car and caravan at weekends, by the way, and certainly not at night. If you keep to daytime and weekdays you will encounter fewer hazards, but even then you will need a great deal of patience for the long climb and even more when you are coming down.

A properly matched outfit should cruise at maximum permitted speeds up hill and down dale on autoroutes, motorways, autobahnen and autostrade. In France the speed limit for caravan towing is 100 k.p.h. (62 m.p.h.) on open roads, no limit on autoroutes.

Deciding upon the size and weight of a caravan in relation to the size and weight of your car is not the whole story, however. You want to be sure that the caravan you have chosen will tow well behind your particular car.

A brief trial marriage between your car and the proposed new caravan is desirable, preferably on roads where a straight run at a good speed is possible. Snaking is a most disconcerting habit that should be predictable but is not. Quality towing is not by any means the prerogative of quality outfits. The only way to be sure is to have a good trial run. If the seller of the caravan is reluctant to allow this you must be equally reluctant to buy.

Nobody can say why some cars tow some caravans better than others. You can adjust the balance, nose-weight etc., with the greatest care and yet caravan 'A' will tow beautifully behind car 'B' but snake behind car 'C'.

A trial run is the answer. If you are unfortunate enough to have an outfit that does not tow well you can try loading the caravan in a different way; if this does not improve matters you can buy stabilizers to dampen lateral movement of your caravan.

Having said all this it must be admitted that many caravanners never seem to bother much about relative weights. If your car has a large boot and you regularly load the heaviest items into this you have gone a long way towards solving the weight distribution problem.

It may be that you are proposing to buy a new car to tow your new caravan. You want the sort of power that will go up the side of a house rather than win the Monaco Grand Prix, in other words with good torque. You want high road wheel torque at low engine revolutions, the Land-Rover probably being the best example. Diesel power is preferable, but there are not many diesel cars.

It is said that automatic transmission provides greater traction, but you should consult your car manufacturer for advice and any modifications necessary before deciding upon the type of caravan you can best tow with an automatic-drive car.

It is comforting to have a low bottom-gear ratio for stopping and starting on hills. I can remember getting stuck with an old Vauxhall Cresta (a splendid car, I thought, until I realized the towing disadvantages of only three gears), towing a Bluebird caravan, I believe; it seems like a hundred years ago but the memory remains. Climbing up the middle road out of Nice, which is not as wide as all that even now, with traffic in solid lines up and down, we were stopping and staggering and stopping and staggering until we simply could not stagger any more. The line of big Continental trucks behind us were delighted, as you can imagine. The moral of this story is that if your bottom-gear ratio is inadequate you will be balked in the most embarrassing situations and never in situations where you have room to manoeuvre your way out. In 'impossible' situations you can only put bricks or blocks behind the caravan wheels, uncouple and turn the caravan round by hand.

I like to imagine that now I am impervious to the trauma of such emergency situations, but the truth probably is that what experience I have gained has minimized them.

Other features making for a good towing car are small rear overhang and firm rear suspension; spring assisters can help with this. A strong chassis frame, a long wheelbase and a wide track are other desirable features to look for in a good towing car.

Do not be put off, however, if your car does not possess all these features. There are so many types of caravan and trailer-tent that whatever car you own you will find one to enable you to enjoy 'le camping'.

If you and your car are new to caravanning you must obviously have a towing hitch fitted to your car, and it must be properly fitted. Some car manufacturers have their own special type of hitch which is supplied and fitted by their authorized agents. You should resist the temptation to allow a well-meaning handyman neighbour to rig something up for you. The hitch should be at the right height for the caravan to ride at a good level.

Whilst the towing hitch is being fitted you might also like to order mud flaps for the rear wheels of the car to protect the front of your new caravan. And do not forget that the caravan will need a number plate bearing the number of your car.

When you set about choosing a caravan the first consideration is to determine the weight your car can tow; then ascertain the models of this weight within your price range. If you are doubtful about towing characteristics following a trial run you could consider hiring a similar model for a week.

Most caravans are 4-berth models. In a great many 4-berth caravans a fifth berth can be squeezed in somewhere as an extra. There are 6-berth and 7-berth caravans but, naturally, larger caravans need larger cars to tow them and larger manoeuvring space and larger muscles if they have to be manhandled and they incur larger car ferry charges.

If you have a large family there is no need to have a berth for each member inside the caravan. Camp beds in attached tent awnings or annexes are admirable.

Should you be thinking of buying a second-hand caravan and are uncertain of its age you can quote the serial number (usually situated on the frame by the jockey-wheel) to the manufacturer who will then tell you the year of manufacture. If you are buying a second-hand caravan privately and wonder if it might still be subject to a hire purchase agreement I understand that your local Citizens' Advice Bureau can check for you if you give them the serial number.

You should not really consider a second-hand caravan which is so second-hand that its lighting does not conform to the present-day requirements of an international two-way socket providing brake lights, indicators, lights and interior lights for the caravan; it is also obligatory to have a flasher unit in your car to tell you that your caravan indicator lights are working.

The most popular size of caravan is between 12 and 15 ft. with a 4-berth layout;

it is much preferred to 2-berth versions. Many of the caravanners we meet abroad are retired, many husband-and-wife-only teams, but in 4-berth caravans, a large number with the double dinette lay-out – at each end a central table with seats on either side, the whole convertible to a double berth. The advantage of this lay-out is that the wife/husband can lie in bed in the morning watching the husband/wife laying the breakfast at the other end of the caravan.

Having decided the size and type of caravan you would like the next thing is to decide on the best interior lay-out. The makers' catalogues set out many variations. When you have narrowed down your choice, your final selection will be influenced by the quality of the fittings and whether they stick out or not, whether the surfaces are of hard-wearing and easy-to-clean materials. Some of the elaborate veneers look magnificent but they are not at all necessary for caravanning comfort.

It is likely that the cooking and washing areas will be covered by fold-away tops. You can never have too many working surfaces in a caravan. The sink and draining-board will probably be a one-piece plastic moulding in the less expensive caravans, but made of stainless steel in the dearer models.

Tables usually unclip to form the base for beds, seating cushions and back rests double up in ingenious fashion as bunk mattresses. The tables that form bed bases should be a good fit so that gaps do not appear during your hours of sleep.

The extra beds provided by canvas bunks stretched on fitted rods are splendid for children but rather small for adults.

A tent extension or awning, already mentioned, doubles your living area and is easy to erect; most caravans have a groove or awning tracks around the outside edge on the door side; in this groove the inside edge of the awning is run, extended outwards by a framework and secured in the ground like a tent. A canvas draught excluder clips over the wheel. British caravanners seem to go in for these extensions only when sleeping facilities overflow, but foreign caravanners use them as extensions of living space; in hot weather they act like a cool enclosed porch of a front door. They are useful as bedrooms, dining-rooms, kitchens and play areas on wet days, being fitted with plastic windows and roll-up screens.

A tent awning is of particular value with a motor-caravan because it provides a living area that motor-caravans lack; which brings us to the question that concerns most beginners to caravanning: should they go in for a caravan or a motor-caravan?

You should not automatically assume that it is easier to drive a motor-caravan than to tow a caravan, particularly if your car, that you are used to, is capable of towing. Many people confess to being scared of towing a 'great big van' behind them; they think that the alternative of driving a motor-caravan would be just like driving a car, which it is not. The relatively high-up position of the driver's seat, over and often ahead of the front wheels, can be disconcerting on the trial run, perhaps on hard plastic commercial cab seats and with an underpowered engine. Getting up to a reasonable speed can be quite a haul, the bounce at the front can be unnerving and the proximity to danger alarming.

After a disappointing trial run in a motor-caravan I have known people give up the idea of caravanning altogether because they imagine that towing a caravan would be even worse. As the song says, 'it ain't necessarily so'. The familiarity of your own car is an important factor and your first reaction to towing a caravan is that your car has become sluggish; after this initial strangeness, most experienced motorists have no problems when they tow for the first time. Obviously you have to take into account the width of your caravan when steering through narrow gaps in traffic and passing cyclists but you soon get used to this; for instance, at first you seek petrol only in wide forecourts, but after a little experience you realize that it is a simple matter to pull in anywhere.

Pull in for petrol anywhere

Reversing, admittedly, needs practice. With practice you realize that you have a 'seeing' side and a 'blind' side, and you manoeuvre into position accordingly so that reversing loses its fears. It is helpful if a passenger gets out to 'see you back' and even more helpful if they stand where you can see them. With many caravans it is necessary for someone to get out to pull back the brake over-ride lever before you can reverse, but more recent caravans have an automatic mechanism for this. There is never any need to panic when reversing even if you set up a 'jack-knife' situation; all you need to do is move forward to straighten up and start again. It is a good idea to practise with models on a table top so that you can see exactly how a caravan reacts to the manoeuvring of a car.

A variation of caravan and tent that you see on sites everywhere abroad is the trailer tent. This is a trailer in the shape of an oblong box about 7 ft. long, 5 ft. wide and 3 ft. high that can be towed behind the smallest car because its weight is around 6 cwt. (Not that its use is restricted to small vehicles for you see quite luxurious cars towing trailer tents.)

The top opens up and folds back, thereby almost doubling its length, and this action draws up out of the trailer a tent and framework and more folds of tent in which are windows and a door, like a magician producing from a hat far more than you imagine could be accommodated there. The body length is transformed

Trailer tent, ready for the road

from 7 ft. to 13 ft., the width from 5 ft. to 13 ft. and the height from 3 ft. to 8 ft. And these dimensions describe but a *small* trailer tent!

Some of the trailer tents are as expensive as caravans but, of course, cannot have caravan fittings such as wardrobes built in, although they do have built-in kitchens. Principal advantages of the trailer tents are that they tow much more easily than a caravan – in fact you are hardly aware that you have a trailer tent behind your car; they scarcely affect the petrol consumption of the car and car ferry charges are much less than for a caravan.

To return to the comparison of caravan versus motor-caravan: a motor-caravan is handier, cheaper on car ferries and often on sites, but it costs as much to buy as a car and caravan together, and sometimes more.

If you are planning to explore the mountain regions of France a motor-caravan will be more suitable because it will be less nerve-racking than a caravan to manoeuvre around hairpin bends and on precipitous passes.

If you are the sort of person who is always anxious to get on you will be better off with the easier 'get-up-and-go' advantages of a motor-caravan. And your long-suffering passengers can at least recline in a motor-caravan whereas they are not allowed to travel in a caravan.

Arriving at a site in a caravan you can leave it on your allotted pitch whilst you

Trailer tent, erected

go off in your car to explore; arriving at a site in a motor-caravan you vacate your pitch when you go off exploring – a tent awning that you can leave behind to stake your pitch in your absence is an advantage here.

Motor-caravans need more manoeuvring to level up than caravans.

When holidays are over you are more likely to get more occasional and spontaneous use out of a motor-caravan during the rest of the year; odd weekends away are more easily undertaken with a motor-caravan for parking space is easier to find.

These are just a few considerations. After many years' experience I suspect that caravanners are caravanners and that motor-caravanners are motor-caravanners, taking to their choice by an instinctive preference that lies beyond argument or persuasion, just as sailing sailors buy yachts and motoring sailors buy motor-cruisers.

It is my impression that in France you do not see anything like the number of French-owned motor-caravans as you see British or American; perhaps I am hypnotized by watching so many French trailer tents unfold that my impressions are unreliable.

A final word: before you buy a caravan make sure that you have somewhere to keep it; if at home make sure that there is no bye-law to prevent your parking it.

4 FIXTURES, FITTINGS AND EQUIPMENT

Other things being equal (which they seldom are), your final decision in choosing a caravan will depend upon the variety and quality of fixtures, fittings and equipment.

An item that might be mentioned first is that unmentionable subject of toilet facilities; this aspect of caravanning, you may or may not be surprised to learn, has put some people (British, needless to say), off the very idea in the past.

Chemical toilets have been available for years; it would not really be true to say that they have been popular for years. With the arrival of portable flush toilets some embarrassments have been diminished, and where adequate space is provided in a caravan toilet compartment equipped with a portable flush toilet there is no need for any embarrassment at all. It is a waste of precious floor area to provide ample space that is so rarely used and the extending toilet compartment is an excellent solution. Some caravans double up the use of the toilet compartment as a shower department; this is an unnecessary luxury in France where, on the majority of sites, the toilet and shower facilities are excellent, even if it is not always considered necessary to segregate the sexes.

Also, on French sites, there is invariably provision, clearly marked, for the emptying of portable toilets. Foreigners carry their toilet containers to the emptying-point at any old time, but if, being frightfully British, you prefer the dead of night, do be careful not to spill any of the recharging liquid on your hands.

The majority of toilet and shower blocks on French sites are excellent and, far from being an embarrassment, it is a delight to wander to and from the showers in your dressing-gown, breathing in the beautiful morning air. Everybody else does.

Most shower blocks in France also have dish-washing and clothes-washing sections, with free hot water, metered hot water or no hot water. After a big meal it is easier to load the washing-up into a couple of buckets to wash in comfort at the shower block than to struggle on the limited working-top spaces of your caravan.

Water in the caravan is obviously limited. The tap at the sink is operated by a foot or hand pump, drawing the water from a container, usually a 5-gallon plastic

A delight to wander from the showers in your dressing-gown

drum, inside or outside the caravan. The 5-gallon drums of water are quite enough to carry and they need filling several times a day.

If the container is kept outside the caravan the pipe leading into it should have an 'insect cap' if your container is not to become the local swimming-pool for insects. You will soon appreciate the necessity of keeping the container(s) under the caravan in the cool. Some caravans have built-in storage tanks; this is an advantage only if you prefer going off on your own, away from sites. All sites in France have good water; there is no need for your car to haul water from one site to another. Simply carry enough in a container for your needs en route.

The sink and the washbasin drain to a pipe running outside the caravan under which you place your waste bucket.

At many sites in France electricity is provided. On arrival you are asked if you need an electricity supply and, if so, you are directed to the 'wired' pitches, usually in a group. Some of the better caravans are wired to provide electric cooking, refrigerator (which does not protect food when on the move, of course), lighting, heating, hot water and even a washing machine.

Before considering the use of any electrical equipment from mains supply the caravan must be properly wired. For warm weather caravanning an 'electric' caravan has no special advantage in France because the majority of sites are well equipped with every facility. If you propose winter caravanning, or to go to ski resorts, an 'electric' caravan is to be preferred; in these circumstances you also need insulation.

Normally the walls and roof of a caravan are insulated anyway, but if you are contemplating cold weather touring you need underfloor insulation as well.

Cold nights often follow warm days in France and it is tempting to close all the windows and vents to work up a nice fug. In the confined space of a caravan nothing could be more dangerous; far better to catch a cold than to suffocate, for sleeping bodies and heaters use up oxygen very quickly. Caravan windows and roof-lights are adjustable to stay open at varying apertures. In warm weather you will need them to be open at night and then mosquito screens will be necessary.

Poor ventilation in varying temperatures causes such condensation that bedding can become wet through and caravan walls can run with water. You should watch for condensation under bunk beds at night; you can get over the difficulty by laying newspapers on top of the table-top/bed-bases to take up the moisture. The table tops with heat-resistant surfaces are particularly liable to condensation when being used as bed-bases. Some caravanners close down the roof vents at night in the mistaken belief that the dampness is coming in that way; this is quite wrong and roof-lights should be left open. In fact roof-lights and fixed ventilators should always be left open, particularly when the caravan is left unoccupied.

The type of bedding used is a matter of personal preference. Making up beds with sheets and blankets is rather a fuss and sleeping-bags are often preferred if they are well insulated. It is a big advantage if all the bedding will stow in the lockers under the seats.

The friendly French sun will soon dry bedding that has become wet through condensation, also your washing of course. You will find it a great convenience to carry a clothes-line that you can rig from the caravan to a nearby tree, but on some French sites there are restrictions on clothes-lines and special areas are provided for hanging out clothes. If no guidance is given on arrival you will soon see what others are doing and follow suit. We carry a folding plastic frame for fitting to the outside of one of the windows and this serves admirably for drying 'smalls'.

A carpet is a pleasant luxury and inexpensive in view of the small floor area. You will appreciate it in the mornings when stepping out of bed to make the tea: you will not appreciate it when mud, pine needles etc., are 'walked' into the caravan.

Storage of clothes must be a compromise, for no caravan can provide enough cupboards and lockers; low-down spaces under bunks are used for the stowage of bedding and high-up spaces cannot be fully utilized because high-level stowage affects stability.

Food stowage is not a problem because most meals can be provided on a day-to-day basis, as of course they must be if there is no refrigerator. There are shops on or near many French sites and even sites without shops usually provide bread and milk, also Camping Gaz and postage stamps.

Crockery stowage space is usually shaped and recessed to prevent rattling and breakage; other crockery and cooking utensils are provided with adequate space in

Clipped on the window is a folding plastic frame for drying smalls

the cooking area, but the method of stowage should take into account that the caravan will be bounced around somewhat when moving.

The cooking department in a caravan can either be electric, as already mentioned, or Calor Gas, with which the French Camping Gaz is interchangeable. Most caravans have a two-ring hotplate with a grill, the more expensive models being equipped with ovens as well. Caravanners with only hotplates can enjoy the luxury of roast meat or fowl with a barbecue. Apart from the efficiency of this method of cooking it is fine therapy to sit before the spit, a long-handled spoon in one hand basting the succulent joint as it turns round and round powered by a small battery, and in the other hand a glass of Châteauneuf du Pape. Barbecues are less expensive in this country than in France so that it would pay you to get one before you go. It might also be prudent to practise with it in the safety of your own garden.

We bought our barbecue years ago, at Perpignan I think, and carried it back in triumph to our site that was in rather an exposed position and never really free from the wind. I had bought a beautiful little round of beef, the necessary wine we possessed. There were no caravans near us, but five or six elaborate trailer tents were down-wind. I erected the barbecue on its legs, filled the back 'grate' with charbon, poured on methylated spirit, flung on a lighted match. Immediately a

34

gale arose, the charbon glowed into a red intensity as though it was hay, a fountain of sparks rocketed skywards like a space probe. I had terrified visions of barbecued trailer tents and leapt up in some anxiety to warn the occupants. To my great relief I saw that the sparks were dying almost as soon as they were airborne. I quickly rigged a screen to windward to lessen the draught and set the skewered beef a-turning. The cooking time for the weight of beef was an hour and a half and my wife had asked for notice to peel and cook potatoes and vegetables. We were eating in ten minutes, just beef by itself. Since then I have taken the trouble to master the art of barbecuing.

Open fires and barbecues are prohibited in summer on some sites and in all forest areas in France. Another splendid alternative is a pressure cooker, also a container on non-pressure lines known as a waterless cooker. With either a complete meat and vegetable meal can be quickly prepared on one burner.

Lighting in most caravans is provided by gas, which is reliable and economical. It is as well to carry a stock of spare mantles for they are shaken about when on the move. Some caravans have fluorescent tube lighting run from the car battery and others have a secondary electrical lighting system built in.

Some form of refrigeration is necessary, particularly in the sultry heat of the south of France; milk and food simply cannot stay fresh without cooling assistance. You can have food safes cut in the caravan floor, protected from dust but exposed to a cooling draught of air when you are going along; or a container that cools by water evaporation; or an insulated ice-box. None is as efficient as a refrigerator.

Gas refrigerators work on a small 'pilot'-size light, but obviously only work when the light is on. We like to turn off the gas supply at night and when we are on the move so that a gas refrigerator in France is of little use to us. The point of turning off the gas at the bottle is to eliminate the possibility of gas escape; we could, of course, use one gas bottle for the refrigerator only so that alone could be left on when the supply to the other appliances was turned off. If the refrigerator gas light was blown out accidentally a fail-safe device would turn off the supply.

Electric refrigerators can be left on at night without worry, but clearly are of no use on a 'non-electric' site or when you are on the move. If you stay on one site for any length of time and stock up with perishable food as soon as the electricity supply is connected this type of refrigerator is adequate.

Electric refrigerators run from their own battery are a better bet, or from the car battery. Best of all are the refrigerators that work from a 12 v battery and/or from gas.

Camping Gaz bottles or cylinders (6 lb.) are available at many caravan sites and almost everywhere in shops in France. Most caravans have a 2-bottle stowage in front of the body on the towing frame, clamped on and with provision for pad-locking, or enclosed.

The time that a bottle lasts varies considerably from family to family, but if you have two full Calor bottles (10 lb. each) when beginning your three-week holiday in France they should certainly last out. Try not to take one that is almost empty for it is a waste to give a weighty Calor Gas bottle a free ride round France. Calor/ Camping Gaz adaptors are obtainable at any caravan shop. If you run out of Calor Gas in France you will have to buy a Camping Gaz container; you can do nothing with your Calor container or bottle except bring it back since seeking out a 're-charging' station is rarely worth the fuss. So that your first purchase of Camping Gaz will have to include the container, which will not leave you with much change out of five pounds (as in England, of course, when first buying Calor). If you have to buy a Camping Gaz cylinder in France you will find it cheapest to do so at one of the big supermarkets; once you have the container you can renew anywhere.

We usually set off with Camping Gaz cylinders only, because we stay abroad beyond the length of time that Calor bottles would last.

Calor/Camping Gaz is safe if you look after it. If you suspect a leak, rub liquid shampoo or soapy water over the connections; where there is a leak it will bubble. Do not look for a leak with a lighted match. It is not advisable to smoke when changing cylinders, nor to stow full cylinders in any position other than upright. If, through negligence or accident, a fire occurs, turn off the main valve on the top of the cylinder.

You must have one or two fire extinguishers by the cooker for dealing with small outbreaks or cooking disasters. If you are unfortunate enough to have a fire that develops beyond the capacity of your extinguisher you should get everybody out of the caravan quickly. But this very rarely happens, I am glad to say.

You will probably take pots and pans with you from home, although the three-in-one saucepans that go on one hot-plate are a great help in the limited cooking area of a caravan.

Lightweight folding chairs and a table should be taken; most caravanners in France take their meals outside and it is very pleasant.

A first-aid box is a useful safeguard and knowing how to use it, a comfort when you are a long way from familiar emergency services; not that you need have any doubt about the adequacy of medical services in France. The camp site office will give you details of the nearest doctors and dentists, summon aid and very often help you in your own language. You have to pay doctors and dentists for their services and chemists for their prescriptions, but such items are recoverable from the holiday insurance that you should take out before leaving. Most British holiday-makers abroad qualify for reciprocal health benefits under the 1973 EEC Social Security regulations. Before you begin your holiday you should apply to a Department of Health and Social Security office or an Employment Exchange for Form E.111.

Ours is a healthy life though and few caravanners have need to resort to the excellent health services. Camp sites are healthy because the majority are well run in France with daily refuse disposal and cleaning of toilet blocks. You would be most unpopular if you disposed of your waste anywhere other than in the appointed places. Disposable waste bin liners are the simplest for caravan life.

In thinking of odd items necessary to the enjoyment of a French caravan holiday I suppose that at the top of the list would come a corkscrew; spare gas mantles have already been mentioned; aerosol insecticides should be taken and favourite lotions for dealing with insect bites; stick-on coat hangers, gum-boots, a spade, electric torches (some sites turn out lights at night), a whistling kettle (to summon the duty tea-making slave), a wind-break, sun awnings (the French caravan window awnings are the best), and a spirit level. Levelling up the caravan properly takes only a short time; for years I was very casual about this until one day a bottle of Côtes de Provence slid from a polished surface and smashed on the floor. I bought a spirit level immediately and have used it ever since.

Your caravan adventure in France can be such a wonderful experience that it is a pity to spoil the holiday for a ha'porth of equipment.

One item of equipment that I do *not* consider to be worth the bother of carrying is a boat. You see boats hoisted aloft on roof racks (a potential 'high vehicle' charge indeed on the car ferries), but you can be certain that a boat big enough to be worth taking is too big and heavy to transport in this way whilst a boat light enough for convenient transport is too small for safety on the water.

5 PREPARATIONS–ON THE ROAD

You should have an International Camping Carnet because a number of sites in France will not let you in without one; this is understandable since the Carnet is supposed to be an indication that you are an 'approved' caravanner with the necessary Third Party cover. By depositing your Carnet you are freed from the necessity of depositing your passport.

Carnets are issued by the A.A., Camping Club, Caravan Club, Motor Caravanners' Club, R.A.C., and the Touring Club de France. Some sites claim to offer discounts to holders of the Carnet, though not in season nor for short stays; reasons other than the prospect of discounts attract caravanners to sites.

If you are a member of one of the motoring organizations they will issue your Camping Carnet, GB plates and international driving permit, if you want one, and also look after your car ferry booking and insurance. The A.A. 'See-you-alright-in-the-event-of-disaster' Service I was very glad to have behind me on one occasion when hauling a heavy caravan in the Savoie-Dauphiné and the long-suffering radiator of my car decided to emulate Stephenson's Rocket. I must admit that it is very comforting when you are far from home to have a helpful telephone number to tell your troubles to. The R.A.C. run a similar scheme and so does the Caravan Club; in fact theirs is probably now the best for caravan owners.

If you have a caravan you can arrange these comprehensive foreign touring facilities and insurance, in addition to the issue of the Camping Carnet, through membership of The Caravan Club Ltd., 65 South Molton Street, London W1Y 2AB.

If you have a motor-caravan you can arrange facilities for your tour, in addition to the issue of your Camping Carnet, through membership of The Motor Caravanners' Club Limited, 22 Chiswick High Road, London W4 1TQ.

For caravanning/camping in France you would expect the Touring Club de France to specialize and, of course, they do.

Whichever body you apply to for your Carnet-Camping International, to give it its correct title, will need a passport-size photograph. Oddly enough, since the Carnet is regarded in a way as a reference, you can buy one abroad at a number of

Book early in the season

the sites requiring you to have one, obviously a cheaper way than joining a club for the sole purpose of getting it.

Your present insurer of car and caravan will attend to the extension of cover necessary for your Tour de France. Let them know if you propose to make brief diversions into neighbouring countries. From 1 January 1974 the Green Card is not officially required when visiting E.E.C. countries but, at the time of writing, insurance companies are still issuing them and, so long as they do, we should presumably carry them.

When you come to book the car ferry, remember that the shorter crossings are naturally the least expensive, Dover–Calais/Boulogne being a good deal less for an average car and caravan, two adults and two children than the cost of the Southampton–Le Havre crossing.

If you live in the West Country you may favour the new Plymouth–Roscoff (near Brest), route.

The consideration of driving to the least expensive ferry crossing is well worth while since you have your hotel with you; against this is the understandable impatience to 'be abroad' at the earliest possible moment.

If you have to take your caravan holiday at the height of the summer you will know that it is necessary to book the ferry well in advance. Out of season there is no need to book either way. You should send for the brochures of all the ferry operators in order to decide which crossing will suit you best.

It cannot be stressed too frequently or too strongly that the best time to caravan through France is out of season. If you are free to go when you like you will find enough permanently open sites at any time and where the climate plus year-round tourist interest attracts year-round visitors you will find a selection of sites open.

In addition to the items mentioned you will need:

Passport: valid to cover the period up to the date of your return.

Car Registration Book: it is safer to take the original; a photostat copy is not always acceptable. If the car is not your own you should carry the owner's written consent to use it.

Full (not Provisional) current **Driving Licence:** if you propose caravanning near the Spanish border and feel that you may be tempted to go on a car excursion into Spain you would be wise to take with you an International Driving Permit (obtainable from the A.A. or R.A.C. for a fee and a passport-size photograph). Similarly, for a trip into Italy you would need a translation slip for your Driving Licence, obtainable from the A.A. or R.A.C., also a red triangle in case of breakdown.

GB Plates on car and caravan, placed near to the number-plates.

Yellow Headlamp and **'Dip-to-the-right' Converters** if you are going to be out at night in France. Yellow is not compulsory for visitors as it is for French cars, but some routiers flash a disconcerting array of headlights against white headlamps; not so much because they are white but because they are elevated, the weight of the caravan at the back of the car beaming the white headlamps into the air. If you propose to drive at night on your tour you will be saved much inconvenience if you check your headlamp alignment with the caravan hitched on before you go. Some cars, French ones particularly, as you probably know, have adjustable beams.

Extending driving mirrors so that you can *really* see traffic behind your caravan. The 'clip-on' variety tend to vibrate out of focus. The central periscope-type rear mirror is excellent.

And last, but by no means least:

Money: there is no need to bother so much now about taking your estimated money requirements in money or Travellers' Cheques. Your own bank Cheque Card entitling you to draw up to £30 a time is acknowledged everywhere in France. It is only necessary to make sure that you have enough cheques in your cheque book before you go.

If you propose staying abroad for more than a month you can return your motor tax disc to your Motor Taxation Department for a refund in respect of each clear month that you will be abroad. Have a letter and envelope ready to post your tax disc from your port of embarkation.

Your car will be raring to go, serviced and in peak condition for its toughest test of the year; you will have thought to include a kit of spare parts, fan belt etc. Caravans need checking over too, preferably from time to time at the works of the local dealer; but you can ensure that the automatic braking is working properly, that all chassis nuts are tight, that the tyres are in good condition and that the coupling is well greased and suitably covered with a cap to protect your clothes.

You drive down the ramp on to the car ferry. You may stay hitched on or you may not; if the type of ferry, or loading arrangements, requires your caravan to be uncoupled it will be expertly disconnected and wheeled aside almost before you can look into the driving mirror to see that it is no longer there. Some car deck sections are 6 ft. high so watch impulsive roof-rack loading.

Parked on Dieppe front after a night crossing

On arrival at the French port you will be singled out of line on the car deck and your caravan will quickly be hitched on. You drive off the ferry into France, feeling a little strange at being on the right-hand side of the road, and your adventure has begun. The only problem about driving on your near side of the road is when overtaking; apart from this it is an advantage when judging distances to the side of the road and sometimes to the *edge* of the road on mountain passes. If it happens to be night-time when you leave the car ferry do not attempt to make progress right away in unfamiliar driving conditions and on the 'wrong' side of the road. Pull in at any parking place and stop for the night. You will not be disturbed and it is important that your first drive through France should be in daylight.

Make a point of checking after every stop that your brake lights and indicator flashers on the caravan are working; it is a simple drill for your passenger to check before you move off.

Most accidents involving British drivers occur within a hundred miles or so of the Channel ports (both going and coming), so take it easy at first. A big percentage of accidents happen when pulling away from a halt sign at cross-roads; you look right and then left, but instinctively you look left across to the far side of the road and can easily overlook the danger of fast traffic coming up close to you on the right-hand side of the road and sometimes partly obscured by your passengers.

The 'mile' posts are kilometre posts now; to convert kms into miles multiply by five and divide by eight. On main roads you have priority over traffic entering from side roads, but in towns, traffic coming from your right has priority. This can be most disconcerting until you get used to it, but the signs are clear enough, 'Priorité à Droite' means 'Give way to traffic from the right' and 'Passage Protégé' means that you have priority. The international sign of a red diamond is spaced out on priority roads and also a black on yellow diamond meaning the same thing; a black bar across this sign means the end of the priority section.

The first thing to establish as you get under way is that you can really see in your rear mirrors the traffic coming up behind you. If there is some obstruction in the caravan that is preventing what would otherwise be a see-through view, or if your extending mirrors are not in proper alignment, pull off the road at the first opportunity to adjust. No other factor contributes so much to driving anxiety with a caravan abroad than the inability to see what is overtaking you; and some traffic comes up from behind really fast, not only cars but vast trucks with trailers too. Apart from the danger of pulling out into overtaking traffic, it is helpful to note when you are about to be overtaken by high-sided trucks which exert a 'sway' on the caravan. If you see them coming you can be prepared for it.

Road markings of solid lines and dotted lines on either side of solid lines are similar to British road markings except that they are usually painted yellow. When you decide to overtake, obviously in an overtaking section, flash your indicators in good time and *go*, pulling back in when your caravan is well clear of the overtaken vehicle. British drivers are inclined to dither, particularly when abroad and particularly when towing. At roundabouts French drivers accept their right of way almost without looking, and often completely without looking. If you dither at a roundabout to wonder if a French driver is going to concede you your right of way you may depend on it that he will not.

Having established that you can see clearly behind you the next point to be quite happy about is that your caravan is towing well. Sometimes foldaway beds have not been lowered, causing slight loss of balance, or something heavy might have been left at the rear of the caravan causing it to be nose-light. If your steering feels too light it means that you have too much weight forward in the caravan so that it is nose-heavy. If your steering feels too heavy it means that the rear of your caravan is overloaded making it nose-light. If everything appears to be in order and yet you are not satisfied with the towing characteristics, try putting another 3 lb. of pressure in the rear car tyres.

It takes very little time and effort to ensure that your outfit is towing well and once you are settled and relaxed you will be surprised at the distances you can cover on the splendid French roads. On the autoroutes, if your outfit moves nicely at sixty miles an hour you will cover sixty miles in every hour without effort. Unless you have determined upon a driving pattern beforehand the danger is that you will be tempted to drive for too long without a break. My wife and I take turns at driving, changing over every two hours.

Autoroute lay-bys are conveniently spaced and they mostly have toilets and picnic tables. Parking overnight in autoroute lay-bys is not officially encouraged, although you see many motor-caravans and caravans doing so at the height of the summer. A more convenient stopping-place is in one of the rest areas of the petrol station/restaurant-cafeteria parking zones, though tents are not allowed. You can also use the stop to fill up with petrol or to have a snack or breakfast.

Stopping overnight in the lay-bys of ordinary roads in France is not allowed. Stopping with your caravan in the streets of towns is not allowed even if it were possible. For ordinary car parking (without the caravan), you may need a disc unless

You can often park quite easily in smaller towns like Riberac

parking meters are in use. Many French garages supply discs free. In small towns you are often able to park with your caravan in car parks.

Road signs follow the International Code and are much the same as our own. Look out, particularly, for the red ring sign enclosing a caravan. I missed this once in Toulouse when we were channelled off into a narrow, car-width diversion with enclosing pavements on either side. Cars behind started hooting and presently we came to a low archway ahead. I stopped and got out of the car, expecting to see angry fists waving at me from the drivers behind; but they were laughing, raising their arms in 'Ah! the English!' gestures of despair and already reversing.

Archways and bridges show their height in metres, which is splendid so long as you are carrying in your mind the height, in metres, of your caravan. When you ascertain this figure for your car-ferry booking form it is a good idea to note it prominently on your dashboard. When you need it you need it quickly.

A red circle enclosing a trailer means no entry to a trailer and that means a caravan. Where signs indicate an alternative route for heavy traffic (POIDS LOURDS), it is as well to follow this when towing.

Traffic lights are sometimes placed high up in the middle of the road, but mostly they are placed in a similar position to our own. They follow our own pattern of change for stopping if not for starting.

Driving your caravan through France is a delight. You accept the increased amount of gear-changing and soon get the feel of smoothly accelerating up through the gears; you soon appreciate that your stopping distance is much greater and keep a good space between you and the vehicle ahead. This ample space that you leave ahead of you is also appreciated by overtaking vehicles. When the road is too narrow or hilly or winding to allow vehicles to overtake you, and you see in your rear mirrors a build-up of frustrated overtakers, you should get off the road briefly as soon as you can to allow the accumulation of following cars to clear.

The many caravanners we have spoken to on French sites have one big regret in common . . . that they did not take up the wonderful life of caravanning through France before. The big surprise, generally, was the way in which expected driving problems turned out to be non-existent.

6 FRENCH CARAVAN SITES

The British tow into the French site in their Rover; if shown a pitch they drive to it, if not shown one they appear to take any old pitch, back in expertly and seem to vanish.

The Germans tow into the French site in their Mercedes; if shown a pitch they might drive to it, if not shown one they cruise around looking for the best site, back in and immediately bring out sun-loungers, lotions, wind-breaks, folding bicycles, footballs, barbecues.

The Dutch tow into the French site; if shown a pitch they request an electricity supply, if not shown one they select a site in the 'electricity supply' section, exactly and economically equidistant from bread, water, toilets, showers, refuse disposal, efficiently erect a tent awning and busily bustle.

The French tow into the French site in their Peugeot 'San-cat'; if shown a pitch they walk to it with the site man and wave their arms, point up at the trees, the sun, the sky, look eyeball to eyeball at the site man whilst their hands supplicate, measure the fish that got away, hold an imaginary skein of wool; if not shown to a pitch they leave their car and walk, striking poses, considering, measuring, gesticulating. 'If we have it this way you see,' 'Ah, but in the morning the sun . . .' 'Or perhaps across the corner like this,' 'Or over there possebl,' 'This way,' 'That way,' 'Or not here at all perhaps.' Finally the caravan is produced and manhandled by the whole party plus the site man on to some improbable location like a rock. A tent awning emerges, a table, chairs, wine, flowers, a meal.

Somehow the British seem to finish up very comfortably without any fuss at all.

There are about four thousand camping sites in France, probably more if you include the very small ones. Sites are classified according to the extent to which they conform to standards fixed by the French Government. These regulations have only been introduced in recent years but the effect of them has been noticeable as facilities at new sites and improvements at old have clearly been aimed at making the site qualify for the highest standards.

SITE CLASSIFICATIONS

	Approximate old equivalents	New standards
	3rd category	★
	2nd category	★★
	1st category	★★★
	Tourist camp-site	★★★★

Facilities necessary to qualify for the various grades: ★ ★★ ★★★ ★★★★

GENERAL ORGANIZATION

	★	★★	★★★	★★★★
1 Density				
maximum number of visitors allowed at one time: 300 persons or 100 plots per 2½ acres	×	×	×	×
sites where each plot must be staked out to cover an area of 100 sq. metres			×	×
2 Drinking water supply				
minimum amount of water consumption per person and per day in litres	40	50	60	70
concreted water supply points	×	×	×	×
3 Access				
hard surfaced roads leading to the main highway	×	×	×	×
roads inside camp suitable for motor vehicles in all weathers during periods site is open	×	×	×	×
dust-free roads		×	×	
tarred roads				×
4 Lighting				
lighting in public parts of site		×	×	×
lighting up at night of all roads inside site			×	×
5 Security				
efficient means of closing site		×	×	×
guarding of site during day		×	×	×
guarding of site during night			×	×

	★	★★	★★★	★★★★
AMENITIES				
1 Properly built public rooms and sanitary installations	×	×	×	×
2 Management office			×	×
3 Rooms for social and public use			×	×
4 Sports grounds:				
recreation grounds		×		
sports grounds with proper equipment			×	×
SANITARY INSTALLATIONS per 100 guests				
1 WC with flush	3	3	3	3
urinals with flush	2	2	3	3
2 Washing sinks:				
for washing up	2	2	2	2
for laundry	1	1	2	2
3 Showers:				
cold showers, with partitions	1	2		
hot showers, with partitions			3	
hot showers in separate cabins				4
4 Washbasins with shelf and mirror:	4	6		
separate washbasins			8	
in separate cabins				8
5 Electric shaving points			3	3	3
6 Large dustbins with lids	4	4	4	4
daily refuse collection	×	×	×	×
MISCELLANEOUS FACILITIES				
1 Safe-keeping for deposit of valuables			×	×
2 Telephones			×	×
3 First-aid kit	×	×	×	×
4 Food supplies on site or close by			×	×
5 Drinks available during high season				×
6 Flower beds and landscaped gardens			×	×
7 Floral arrangements				×

Within this grading system there is bound to be a variation in standards and even the most excellent tend to suffer at the height of the season. Some sites are not worth their star rating, you may think, whilst others seem to be rated too low. We all have different values.

It is not possible to give a reliable comparison of the difference in charges between a *site and a ****site, but as a rough guide you will probably find that the ****site costs about double the *site. Children are usually taken at a reduced rate. The actual location of a site naturally has a bearing on the charge, for you must expect to pay for enjoying a site in exceptionally beautiful surroundings.

Some sites have a minimum charge in season, say for three or five days, when obviously if you book in you will stay for that length of time. Sites that stipulate a minimum stay are often well worth a longer stay.

Out of season you will always get in somewhere at almost any time of day, but you must allow time for finding a site that is open. In season you must start seeking a site in the early afternoon because there will be fewer spaces available, even though more sites are open.

In France you can depend upon it that camping sites are organized for the sort of peaceful co-existence that was meaningful before the words became part of the vocabulary of political humbug. The peace of French sites is a reality, but no enforcers are in evidence; all you can say is that 'le camping' is peaceful because it is peaceful.

There are rules, of course. The motor road into the camp site is barred at about 10 o'clock, after which you leave your car in the car park outside and walk back to your caravan or sleep outside in your motor-caravan. No music, nor any objectionable noise is allowed after about half past ten. No adolescents are allowed to caravan or camp unless accompanied by their parents.

These rules are kept. The man who invented the saying that rules were made to be broken had never been on a camping site in France.

If you think that it sounds dull to go to bed early in absolute peace then you ought to try being dull for a change. Of course the rules are made for the children, but they are appreciated by the adults. And you find yourself complying as, of course, you should. You turn off your car headlights when returning slowly back into the site in the evening; you do not slam car doors; you do not make a noise and neither do your children.

On the first night you notice the silence and you lie as though cocooned in a world of cotton-wool; the stillness draws you down into the deepest sleep and you relax, utterly grateful to your little box on wheels for contriving the most beneficial rest cure.

Many French sites are in landscaped settings and you rarely see acres of caravans packed in flat fields from hedge to hedge without so much as a tree to break the monotony. Groups of caravans are seen on seashore sites, but, apart from these, many French sites seem to have a way of merging their caravans with trees, hedges, bushes and varying ground levels.

Of course there are transit sites by busy main roads, railway tracks, airports and other noisy neighbours, but you can avoid them if you start looking early enough in the day. There are so many sites in France that there are always alternatives.

Some caravanners like to book ahead by post but this is only necessary for peak holiday times in the most popular holiday areas. On a touring holiday it seems that booking ahead is not popular with experienced caravanners. Our experience over many years has been that if you start looking early enough you can always get in somewhere.

When you drive into a site you should temporarily park your outfit out of the way of other camp traffic whilst making inquiries at the Reception or Site Office. There is usually parking space outside the office and also turning space; it is as well to anticipate the possibility of driving back out again and to park accordingly.

If you are staying you will hand over your Camping Carnet and you may be given a numbered plaque or disc to which a loop of string is attached. This number does not denote any particular site; you simply hang it on your caravan to show that you have booked in. Some sites do have numbered pitches but only for identification purposes at the Site Office.

You may be shown to a site or you may be invited to pitch anywhere. A map of the site in the Site Office will show you the location of 'electric' sites, shower and toilet blocks and other facilities.

If possible you will choose level ground, but if you have to pitch on a slope you should do so with the caravan in an up-and-down direction. Sometimes you have the choice of a slope up or a slope down. I am always in favour of parking the caravan with an eye to getting out (for a quick getaway, according to my wife). I would rather manoeuvre up a slope on arrival than leave myself with the manoeuvre on departure when obstructions or bad weather might make the situation more difficult.

You should use the jockey wheel for levelling up and not the corner legs or steadies which are wound down once the level is achieved; and it is achieved much more satisfactorily with a spirit level. It is useful to carry wooden blocks to place under the corner legs so that they do not sink into the ground; you can also buy metal plates for this purpose.

If you are on a windy site you will want the door on the side away from the wind, but the caravan pointing somewhat into it. Pitches sheltered by camp buildings from prevailing winds are usually taken.

When waiting to check in at the Site Office you often hear other new arrivals inquiring whether or not the water for showers is hot. They might as well save their breath for they will always be told that it is. If you are likely to get excited about this aspect the only way to check is to go to the shower block and run a tap before you book in. The quality and condition of the shower and toilet blocks will contribute very much to your satisfaction with the site, but you may take it that the majority of French sites reach a high standard in this respect. At some sites the water is hot only at certain times of the day, at others the supply is coin-operated. The washing facilities vary enormously and in some areas the dish-washing and clothes-washing facilities are in the open, which gives a heartening indication of the usual weather experienced.

In addition to the water supply at the shower blocks there are usually taps at various points around the site.

At some of the municipal sites in France you may find no one in attendance at the site office during the day, but you will probably find a notice saying when it will be open for the collection of fees. In these circumstances you take any vacant pitch. On these municipal sites you often find modern toilet and shower facilities and also a number of what appear to be permanent residents, since municipal sites are in or near towns. You often see special parking areas for caravans that are left from one year to the next; mainly at attractive sites and frequently including a high proportion of British caravans.

Many French sites have shops; if there are none actually on the site you will find them near by or tradesmen will drive around the site at regular hours each day. When booking in at the Site Office you should inquire what shopping facilities are available. At the better sites there are restaurants open during the season, but eating out in France is expensive.

When the time comes to leave you take your number, if you have been issued with one, back to the Site Office, pay your fee and recover your Camping Carnet.

Beginners often ask me the correct drill for coupling up caravan to car and my particular method is as follows; with the caravan brake on and the jockey-wheel lowered so that the wheel is on the ground, check that it is locked down. To wind up the jockey-wheel above the ball-hitch height of the car will entail winding up the rear corner legs and the front legs may also be wound up. When you reverse the car into position you may not judge it accurately at first. You should take it gently and not mind how many times you get out of the car to see how near you are. If your wife is in the habit of 'seeing you back' an agreed banging-on-the-boot code can be immensely helpful. One bang, STOP, two bangs, LEFT HAND DOWN, three bangs, RIGHT HAND DOWN, no bangs, STEADY AS YOU GO. The beauty of this arrangement is that your incompetent manoeuvring can be fully exonerated by the excuse of faulty signalling. Although caravans are fitted with grab-handles for manhandling I am not a believer in this sort of exertion at all except on hard, level surfaces. If you have no objection to manhandling this is the point at which you would release the caravan brake so that the caravan could be manoeuvred until the coupling is over the ball-hitch.

On bumpy, grassy surfaces it is ridiculous to heave and strain to move the caravan to the car when, without any effort whatever, you can move the car to the caravan. Never be pressurized by circumstances into straining and heaving. Only a few months ago we were preparing to leave a site near Rouen and a German outfit, seeing that we were about to move out, manoeuvred to back in as soon as we had gone. I had backed up my car but, on getting out to inspect, considered that I was not quite near enough. I got back into the car, went forward and reversed again. The German gentleman was tapping his foot on his accelerator, which rather slowed me up and I am not the fastest mover at the best of times, so my wife tells me. I wound down the jockey-wheel coupling on to the ball-hitch of the car and, at the critical moment when I was expecting the satisfying clunk, it fell off, angling the caravan in undignified fashion to the ground. I had no intention of being pressurized by these circumstances into lifting it up and on to the ball-hitch; having locked the jockey-wheel I started to wind the caravan up level again. This was too much for the German gentleman, who leapt out of his car, rushed across and with a vast heave hoisted my caravan by the jockey-wheel and dropped it on to the hitch of the car. I felt no strain at all and since he appeared to be older than I am I thought how foolish he was.

But to continue with the routine: once the coupling has clunked into position on the ball-hitch, raise the jockey-wheel as high as it will go and screw it up tightly into position. Then attach the safety chain(s) and connect the electric cable, making sure that it will not drag along the ground. Check lights. Release the caravan brake, if you have not already done so, to manhandle. Check around the caravan to ensure that all windows etc., are closed, doors locked and the step, if not of the retractable variety, is inside. You would be surprised to learn how many caravan steps are left behind.

If you were unfortunate enough to be bogged down in isolation on a marshy site, perhaps after heavy rain, you should not allow the driving wheels to spin until they dig ruts from which the car cannot extricate itself. At the first sign of wheel-spin disconnect the car from the caravan and drive forward to firm ground, join up a tow-rope and pull the caravan clear.

You will rarely have trouble of this nature, but if you do, you usually find that many willing hands appear uninvited to help you.

7 THE COST OF LIVING

Many people tell us how expensive everything is in France, but we spend no more on food than we do in England. We are in the position of the majority of the French population (and any other), in that we have a limited amount to spend. To hear some travellers talk about the *terrible* prices of all food in France you would imagine that every French man and woman must be a millionaire to survive. This is rubbish, of course, and the truth is that, with certain notable exceptions, you can buy in France what you can buy in England at much the same prices.

The people who complain usually admit to having eaten regularly in restaurants, nibbled and supped in pavement cafés and, of course, you can have three or four coffees or beers in your caravan for the price of one that a waiter brings you.

When we caravan abroad we go for at least three months at a time, sometimes longer. Arriving in France we get the impression that prices have increased since we were last there. On our return to England we get the impression that prices have increased since we were last in England.

All prices are always increasing everywhere, but anyone who claims that all French food is always more expensive than all English food has not tried hard enough. It is a question of whether you habitually shop for the food that you would like or for the food that you can afford.

The beautiful displays of meat everywhere are mouth-watering, but if you cannot afford the best beef you will find that liver, fresh minced beef, chops and cutlets are cheaper. Fish is a good buy and chickens are not expensive; if you buy one in an open market make sure that you are not buying a live one.

You find open markets everywhere in France, big and small markets in towns and villages, with fresh vegetables and fresh eggs that really are fresh. You have to eat so why not make a pleasure out of the whole business of food buying and preparing? Some of the French markets extend for miles, the bigger ones selling clothes, crockery, antiques etc., as well as food. The big displays of French cheeses are fascinating and there is so much on view that you would imagine it to be inexpensive which, unfortunately, it is not.

Bread and eggs, milk and vegetables are no more expensive in France. The supermarkets really are super and present no language problems since all prices and weights are clearly marked as in supermarkets everywhere. Prices are expressed 'per kilo', of course, and you soon get used to the idea that a kilo is more than 2 lb.

Practically all supermarkets have big car parks and in some of them, mostly out of town, there is room to tow in your caravan. It is a delight to wheel out your loaded supermarket trolley right alongside the caravan door and to stow your purchases straight from the trolley into the 'kitchen' cupboards.

Supermarkets are generally less expensive than the camp site shops and we usually have a routine of getting in the large weekly supply from them, topping up daily from the camp shops.

Although you are not allowed to stop with your caravan actually in towns you can sometimes pull in at the end of a wide street in a small town when you need

There are open markets everywhere

Wheel out your loaded trolley; supermarket car park

something on tour, walking back to do your shopping. Best value general multiple stores in France are Casino, Monoprix and Prisunic.

Your shopping programme will depend upon whether or not you have a refrigerator; if not, you will have to buy perishable foods daily or in small quantities and this is where the camp shops score. The morning procession for the flûte or baguette is a feature of French camping life; though superior to our own bread, in my opinion, French bread does not keep and you quite often see an evening procession as well.

When you are on the road you are always able to buy bread somewhere, even on Sundays and holidays. If one *boulangerie* is closed it is likely that there will be another one open nearby.

If you wish to eat English-type breakfasts in France you will find that bacon is relatively as expensive as are croissants in England. But no English caravan can forgo the frequent ceremony of the cuppa and it would be wise to bring a quantity of tea with you since it is more expensive in France than in England. We usually load canteen-size tins of tea and coffee in the bottom of the wardrobe; the only other English standby foods we take with us are tins of minced beef and corned beef for emergencies. A tin of powdered milk is also the sort of thing that you never need if you have it but always need if you forget it.

Biscuits, sweets and chocolate are also more expensive in France but they do not feature very largely in our diets in deference to our waistlines. Jam and marmalade come into the same category and they happen to be more expensive in France.

You cannot very well bring butter with you without a refrigerator and you will not want to pay French prices. We prefer margarine from a health point of view

You can sometimes pull in at the end of a wide street

and many familiar brands are available at reasonable prices. Margarine keeps well so that you can take a supply.

The vast displays of wine in the supermarkets are a pleasure; you should try the various blended wines that are obviously much cheaper than the château-bottled. Many of the supermarkets have fill-your-own-bottle machines. Vin ordinaire costs very little for white, red and rosé and there is quite a selection of brands that are blended to a constant 'taste' and at the price you can afford to experiment until you find a brand that you like. V.D.Q.S. wines cost about double, and Appellation Contrôlée wines from rather more than this to anything you care to pay. Gin, brandy, liqueurs and other drinks, with the exception of whisky, are noticeably less expensive than in England.

English and American cigarettes are not particularly cheap, nor are cigars, but pipe tobacco is and so are French cigarettes, Gauloises or Gitanes, if you and the other occupants of the caravan can stand the pungent aroma.

The restaurants and cafés on sites have already been mentioned with the usual caution about the cost of eating out in France. This caution, I hasten to explain, issues from my financial department. If I could afford to look only at the dishes and never at their cost we would eat out in France more often. If you can afford it by all means stroll from your caravan to dinner at some of the superb camp restaurants; if, like me, you have to count the number of francs in your pocket you may well compromise by taking advantage of some of the 'take-away' food shops that many sites are now organizing.

En route there will be occasions when you will want to eat without the bother of cooking. The meals offered in the autoroute restaurants are good value standard menus. Tourist-type cafés, often situated just outside towns, should be avoided, as should any roadside restaurant where there are no French cars outside; conversely you can always be sure of splendid value (which is not the same as saying that it will be cheap), if you go into a restaurant where there are plenty of French cars around. The most reliable, most economical and best value restaurants are those with the red, white and blue sign of the RELAIS ROUTIERS that you see on every road, for there are 3,900 of them in France. Do not be put off by the number of lorries that you see in their car parks. They are transport cafés with a difference; the surroundings may be humble but the food is of good standard.

You may be reluctant to eat in French restaurants because you are unable to understand the menus. With suitable diffidence I recommend a pocket-size book called *French menus interpreted* which gives a translation and interpretation of 1,500 French dishes and is available from Navigator Publishing Limited, 31 Newtown Road, Warsash, Southampton, Hampshire.

You are likely to find that French shops close for a long lunch but are open until quite late in the evening.

As for storage of food in the caravan, tins and packet foods are obviously easiest to stow anywhere. Vegetables can be kept in plastic containers for a short time but butter and meat will need refrigeration. If you have no refrigerator you could possibly manage with an ice box; ice is widely available. In hot weather the only alternative is to buy perishable food as you want it.

Bottles and liquids generally must be prevented from splashing and breakage when on the move. If you can stow a crate under a seat the divisions make excellent bottle stowage.

Here is a short vocabulary for shopping in France:

English/*French*

apple/*pomme*
apricot/*abricot*
artichoke/*artichaut*
asparagus/*asperges*

bacon/*lard*
baker/*boulangerie*
banana/*banane*
beef/*boeuf*
beefsteak/*bifteck*
  (well done/*bien cuit*;
  medium/*à point*;
  rare/*saignant*)

English/*French*

beer/*bière*
beetroot/*betterave*
blackcurrant/*cassis*
bread/*pain*
broccoli/*choux brocolis*
Brussels sprouts/*choux de Bruxelles*
butcher/*boucherie*
butter/*beurre*

cabbage/*chou*
can-opener/*ouvre-boîte*
carrot/*carrotte*
cauliflower/*choufleur*

celery/*céleri*

cheese/*fromage*

chemist/*pharmacie*

cherries/*cerises*

chicken/*poulet*

chop/*côte*

cocoa/*cacao*

cod/*morue*

coffee/*café*

confectioner/*confiserie*

crab/*crabe*

cream/*crème*

cucumber/*concombre*

cutlets/*côtelettes*

duck/*canard*

egg/*oeuf*

figs/*figues*

fish/*poisson*

fishmonger/*poissonnerie*

flour/*farine*

French beans/*haricots verts*

frogs/*grenouilles*

fruit/*fruit*

fruit shop/*fruitier*

grape/*raisin*

grapefruit/*pamplemousse*

grocer/*épicerie*

haddock/*aglefin*

hake/*colin*

halibut/*flétan*

ham/*jambon*

herring/*hareng*

honey/*miel*

ice/*glace*

jam/*confiture*

kidney beans/*flageolets*

kidneys/*rognons*

lamb/*agneau*

lemon/*citron*

lettuce/*laitue*

liver/*foie*

    beef liver/*foie de boeuf*

    calves' liver/*foie de veau*

    lambs' liver/*foie d'agneau*

lobster/*homard*

mackerel/*maquereau*

margarine/*margarine*

marrow/*moelle*

meat/*viande*

milk/*lait*

mushrooms/*champignons*

mussels/*moules*

mustard/*moutarde*

mutton/*mouton*

oil/*huile*

olive/*olive*

onion/*oignon*

orange/*orange*

oysters/*huîtres*

parsnips/*panais*

pastry shop/*pâtisserie*
peach/*pêche*
pear/*poire*
peas/*pois*
pineapple/*ananas*
plaice/*carrelet or plie*
plum/*prune*
pork/*porc*
potato/*pomme de terre*
prawns/*bouquets or crevettes*

rabbit/*lapin*
raspberry/*framboise*
rhubarb/*rhubarbe*

salmon/*saumon*
salt/*sel*
sausages/*saucissons*
slice/*tranche*
snails/*escargots*

sole/*sole*
soup/*potage*
spaghetti/*spaghetti*
spinach/*épinards*
strawberry/*fraise*
sugar/*sucre*
sweetbreads/*ris de veau*

tart/*tarte*
tea/*thé*
tin/*boîte*
tomato/*tomate*
tripe/*tripes*
trout/*truite*
turbot/*turbot*
turnip/*navet*

veal/*veau*
vinegar/*vinaigre*

water/*eau*

8 MISCELLANEOUS INFORMATION

Public Holidays in France

New Year's Day, Easter Monday, 1 May, Ascension Day, Whit Monday, 14 July (Bastille Day), 15 August, 1 November, 11 November, 25 December.

Banks close on these public holidays, also all day on Saturdays (and Sundays needless to say); on weekdays they are open from 9 a.m. to 4 p.m., many closing for an hour or so at lunch-time. In some towns they also close on Mondays.

Post

Mail can be sent to you c/o any Camping Site, many of which have a mail board in the office. The département Postal Number is shown in the Provinces Section. Most site offices sell postage stamps; you can also buy them at tobacconists (TABAC), and, of course, at Post Offices.

Cats and Dogs

Cats and dogs can be brought into France provided that they have either:

1 A certificate of origin and health, dated not earlier than three days before the animal's journey, stating that it comes from a country where there has been no epidemic of rabies for three years and that it has spent at least six months in that country, or has been there since birth.

or 2 A certificate of anti-rabies vaccination stating that the vaccination was given with a vaccine officially administered more than one month and less than six months before entry into France.

Puppies less than three months old and kittens less than six months old may be taken into France upon production of a veterinary certificate confirming age.

But before you consider taking your pet on your caravan tour of France you should find out the quarantine regulations for re-entry into England.

Caravan Hire

You can hire caravans and camping gear from the car ferry companies, who will be pleased to send you details.

You can hire static caravans on many holiday sites in France.

The Syndicat d'Initiative of the main town in the area you prefer will send information.

You can hire horse-drawn caravans at Toulouse. Details from Syndicat d'Initiative, Donjon du Capitole, 31000 – Toulouse.

Weights and Measures

litres	gals		km	miles		kg	lb
1	0·22		1	0·62		1	2·205
2	0·44		2	1·24		2	4·409
3	0·66		3	1·86		3	6·614
4	0·88		4	2·48		4	8·819
5	1·10		5	3·11		5	11·023
6	1·32		6	3·73		6	13·228
7	1·54		7	4·35		7	15·432
8	1·76		8	4·97		8	17·637
9	1·98		9	5·59		9	19·842
10	2·20		10	6·21		10	21·047
15	3·30		15	9·32			
20	4·40		20	12·43			
30	6·60		50	31·07			
50	11·00		100	62·14			

Part II

THE PROVINCES
OF FRANCE

9 ROUTES CONNECTING THE PROVINCES

PARIS AND THE ÎLE-DE-FRANCE   7, 15, 17, 20, 23, 29, 36, 37, 38, 39, 40, 43

NORD–PICARDIE   1, 17, 20, 21, 23, 24, 44

NORMANDIE   1, 2, 15, 42, 43

BRETAGNE   1, 11, 34, 45

VAL DE LOIRE   1, 2, 3, 4, 11, 13, 14, 27, 28, 29, 33, 34, 37, 38, 41, 42, 45, 48

POITOU–CHARENTES   5, 13, 14, 27, 28, 41

LIMOUSIN   5, 22, 48

AQUITAINE   8, 9, 10, 13, 22, 27, 28, 35

PYRÉNÉES   8, 10, 25, 34, 46, 47, 48, 49

CHAMPAGNE   5, 7, 18, 21, 33, 39, 40, 44

ALSACE   39

LORRAINE   5, 26, 33, 39, 40

BOURGOGNE   4, 5, 12, 18, 33, 36, 38

AUVERGNE   1, 5, 16, 22, 25, 38, 41, 46

FRANCHE–COMTE   7, 18, 21, 26

VALLÉE DE RHÔNE   12, 22, 26, 32, 36, 41, 50

SAVOIE–DAUPHINÉ   12, 31, 36, 50

LANGUEDOC–ROUSSILLON   8, 24, 25, 30, 32, 49

PROVENCE–CÔTE D'AZUR   6, 16, 24, 30, 31, 36

RIVIERA–CÔTE D'AZUR   6, 24, 31

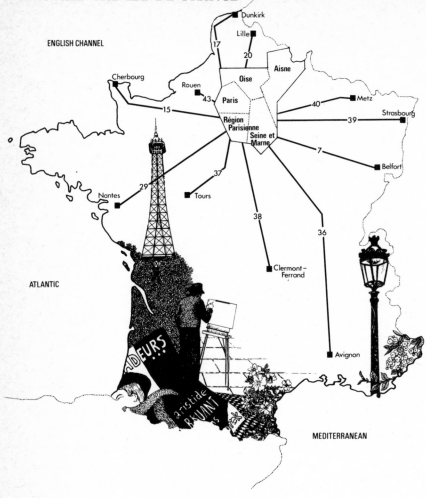

Throughout Part II caravan/camping site seasons are shown as follows:

Caravan/Camping sites printed in lowercase (small) letters, e.g. ★Municipal ★★St. Jean ★★★Le Haut-Dyk ★★★★La Chêneraie, *are open for certain months of each year. Annual guides give a good indication of the current opening dates although they are not 100 per cent reliable.*

Caravan/Camping sites printed in capitals, e.g. ★MUNICIPAL ★★DU PONT ★★★LES PRUNIERS ★★★★CHANTECLER, *are open permanently.*

PARIS and the ÎLE-DE-FRANCE

Approximate number of camping sites 60

Post no.	Département
75	Paris, Seine
92	Hauts-de-Seine
93	Seine-St. Denis
94	Val-de-Marne
95	Val-d'Oise
77	Seine-et-Marne
91	Essonne
78	Yvelines/Seine-et-Oise

Routes connecting   7, 15, 17, 20, 23, 29, 36, 37, 38, 39, 40, 43

The Île-de-France is the area around Paris known as the heart of France, an area representative of all France and the guardian of French history.

With your caravan on a convenient site in or near Paris you can explore the major attractions of the Île-de-France, for all are within a few hours' drive.

Obviously you would not consider exploring Paris with your caravan in tow and you would not be popular if you did so, any more than you would be in any other large city.

If you are staying in the Paris area the most central camping site is the ★★★★BOIS-DE-BOULOGNE, a Touring Club de France site by the Seine, between the Bois-de-Boulogne and the river, the nearest bridge for identification purposes being the Pont de Suresnes. This site is only a quarter of an hour away by car from the Place de la Concorde, but it is often crowded and is not the most restful place by any means; perhaps you would not expect it to be since it is actually in Paris. You are tucked in fairly close to your neighbour, who could be simply anybody, for this must be the most truly international camping site in the world. A mini-bus runs from the site to PONT DE NEUILLY METRO (LINE 1 – Château de Vincennes).

The other T.C.F. Paris site is the ★★★★PARIS-EST-LE-TREMBLAY at Champigny-sur-Marne, from which you will gather that it is on the River Marne. South-east of Paris the Le-Tremblay site is near the race-course of the same name. It is less crowded and less strenuous somehow than the Bois-de-Boulogne site.

A pleasant site by the River Seine is at Maisons-Laffitte, very convenient because it is near to a railway station that is only a quarter of an hour away by the frequent train service from the Gare St. Lazare which, as you know, is right in the most interesting part of Paris. This camping site, the ★★★★MAISONS-LAFFITTE INTERNATIONAL, is in a pleasant situation and is most convenient as a base from which to visit Paris and the Île-de-France.

The best-known landmark

There are many guide-books describing what you should see, but at the top of most lists are the Arc de Triomphe, the Louvre and Versailles. To cover all the recommended excursions would take three weeks of nine-to-five sightseeing, not counting female diversions into the Galeries Lafayette and other tempting distractions. You obviously have to make your personal choice; a dozen lists of sightseeing recommendations might all be different and all of interest. However, here is one selection for the Île-de-France:

Rambouillet: Château; forest with pretty villages; National Sheepfold, stag-hunts with pink-coated riders.

Chartres: Cathedral.

Maintenon: Château de Maintenon with its vast gardens.

Louveciennes: Château of Madame du Barry.

La Celle-St.-Cloud: Château of Madame du Pompadour.

Rueil: Château de la Malmaison where Napoleon lived with Josephine.

L'Hay-les-Roses: Finest rose garden in the world.

Fontainebleau: Forest and château.

Compiègne: Forest; palace; Franco-American Museum.

Beauvais: Cathedral.

Chantilly: Forest; château; race-course (and perhaps to buy some lace and some cream).

There is no particular traffic problem for the caravanner who wishes to pass through Paris now there is the splendid four-lane, fast circular road round it (by comparison with which the circular road around London resembles a goat-track). Coming into Paris you join the Boulevard Périphérique and stay on it until you identify the sign to take you off. Do not be tempted by other signs and be patient if the one you need seems to be a long time showing up. If you seek the comforting signs confirming that you are on the right road you will look in vain. If you are going south you must stay on the Boulevard Périphérique until you actually see the Autoroute du Sud, A.6. sign, ignoring all others.

Although only three camping sites have been named in Paris you will see that there is a choice of fifty or so in the Île de France and you will not have difficulty in finding a site once you select a location. In the ROUTES Section you will find Camping Sites named at COMPIÈGNE on Route 44, RAMBOUILLET on Route 29, NEMOURS, beyond Fontainebleau, on Routes 36 and 37 and MEAUX, on the Marne, on Route 40.

Others are:		Km. from **Paris**
at **Neuilly-sur-Marne** on N.34	**Municipal	14
at **Villennes-sur-Seine** on N.13	****DES RENARDIÈRES (Caravans only)	30
at **Conflans-Ste.-Honorine** on N.14	***la Forêt	25
at **L'Isle-Adam** on N.1	**LES TROIS SOURCES	26
at **Asnières-sur-Oise** on N.309/N.1	**DES PRINCES	35
at **Croissy-Beaubourg** on N.303/N.4	****CROISSY-PLAGE CARAVANNING (Caravans only)	25

NORD — PICARDIE

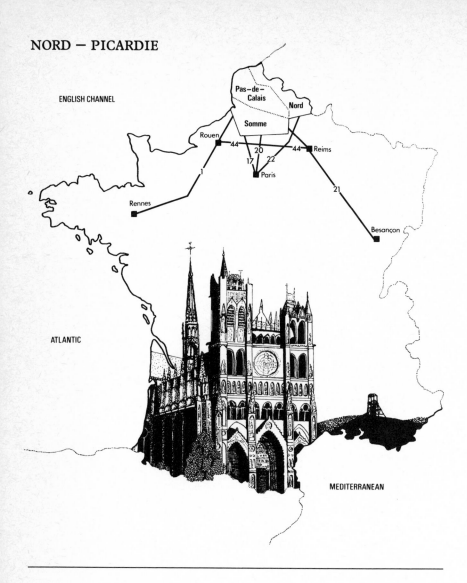

ENGLISH CHANNEL

Pas–de–
Calais

Nord

Somme

Rouen

44

20

17

22

44

Reims

1

Paris

21

Rennes

Besançon

ATLANTIC

MEDITERRANEAN

NORD - PICARDIE

Approximate number of camping sites 160

Post no.	Département	Capital
62	Pas-de-Calais	Arras
59	Nord	Lille
80	Somme	Amiens
02	Aisne	Laon
60	Oise	Beauvais

Routes connecting 1, 17, 20, 21, 23, 24, 44

The holiday attractions for caravanners are mainly on the beaches; inland Nord-Picardie is an area of heavy industry but there are sites situated within range of the big cities and along the Belgian border. It is a province at the cross-roads of Europe, of great masterpieces of Gothic art, of canals and grey skies.

Holidaymakers often think of Picardie, Artois and Flanders as a succession of mining towns, slag-heaps and factories but, in fact, the towns are clean and bright and possess great cathedrals and museums that are amongst the most splendid in France.

For older people there is a great deal of sentimental interest in the battlefields and memorials of the First World War. Second World War veterans take a greater interest in the memorial at Dunkirk.

Malo-les-Bains and Bray-Dunes, with their miles of sands and promenades and camping sites, are probably the best holiday resorts for caravanners in Nord. In Pas-de-Calais there are sands too, but cliffs and dunes as well with many more resorts along the coast, the best-known being Le Touquet.

Inland the main tourist attraction is the beautiful cathedral at Amiens. The country around is a market garden area and there are, of course, many reminders of the First War. There are convenient camping sites along the Somme for anyone interested in visiting the memorials and cemeteries; there is usually parking space for cars and caravans near them.

It may not seem much like a holiday adventure to visit a cemetery, but you should try to make the effort to do so. The gardens are always immaculate, and the names of the regiments and the ages shown on the headstones, the ages particularly, are quite moving.

Nord-Picardie is an area that many caravanners pass through but few explore, entering or leaving France without being aware of the fine sands extending from Belgium to the Seine. Attractive though the coastal area may be it is too near home for the caravanner to consider; having paid to bring his outfit across on the car ferry he can only justify the expense by adding a considerable mileage to it. The

A great deal of sentimental interest ... Rosières

province of Nord-Picardie provides the start and finish of the caravan tour, it is simply a transit stop; in fact where car ferries arrive and depart in the dark it is usual to see caravans parked just anywhere, on promenades and in car parks. Officialdom in France seems to be much more tolerant of this than officialdom in England.

Out of town camp sites fill up according to their distance from the ferry terminal; there are sites on, or near to, most of the main roads leading to and from the terminal ports.

At the end of the holiday some caravanners return to their port a few days early 'to be sure of being there', to relax after the long haul up from the south and to gather strength for the final lap home.

NORMANDIE

Approximate number of camping sites 190

Post no.	Département	Capital
50	Manche	St.-Lô
14	Calvados	Caen
27	Eure	Evreux
61	Orne	Alençon
76	Seine-Maritime	Rouen

Routes connecting 1, 2, 15, 42, 43

Normandie is a beautiful province of wooded countryside, pastureland and splendid beaches, with historical evidence of the Norman conquest of England and of the Allied landings in Normandy all conveniently accessible. The biggest concentration of camping sites is on the coast between Cherbourg and Le Havre. From the ★★★MUNICIPAL site at Bayeux the Bayeux Tapestry and the Invasion Museum are within convenient distance.

This stretch of coast is very popular in the summer though not so much with English caravanners. Coming in to Le Havre the average car ferry traveller is so engrossed with the prospect of his impending dash to the Mediterranean that he is not aware of one of the most fashionable resorts in Europe almost within view, over there to his right. Deauville is a millionaire and movie-star resort, particularly during the August horse-racing, a place in which to stand and stare, but on either side are less sophisticated resorts.

Caen is known as the 'city of spires' and this area certainly attracts many former Allied soldiers who fight the invasion campaign again, with maps and mementoes spread all over the caravan table for the benefit of wives and children. You see motor-caravans with US number plates along by the landing beaches of Omaha and Utah and by the American cemetery at Saint-Laurent.

The top tourist attraction of Normandie is Mont-St.-Michel on the other side of the Cherbourg Peninsula. There are many convenient sites and the thousands of caravanners who use Cherbourg should seriously consider the small detour involved in visiting this 'Wonder of the West'.

One of the most beautiful liqueurs, Bénédictine, is made at the fishing port of Fécamp. The fiery apple brandy, Calvados, is made in the valley of the Auge.

At Rouen the cathedral is the main attraction; it is not often visited by caravanners because stopping nearby is not easy; in fact items of interest are often overlooked in what one might call transit towns for, with a caravan in tow, you have to concentrate on keeping in the right traffic lane for the through route. In addition you would be foolish and most unpopular if you towed the caravan into the old towns

NORMANDIE

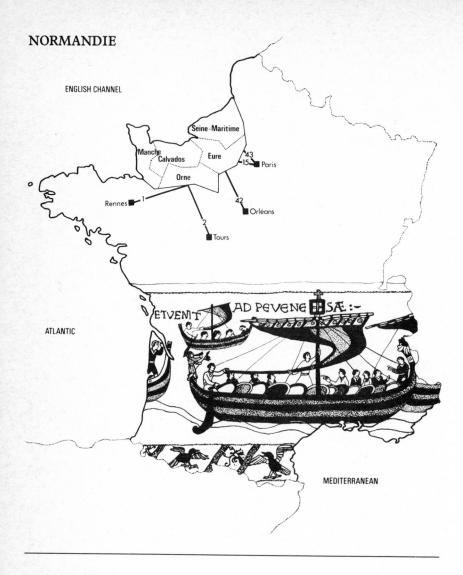

ENGLISH CHANNEL

Seine-Maritime

Manche
Calvados   Eure
              43
              15 ■ Paris
Orne

Rennes ■ 1

        42
        ■ Orléans

2
■ Tours

ATLANTIC

ETVENIT AD PEVENE SÆ:-

MEDITERRANEAN

---

where the sights of greatest historical interest often are. There are a few camping
sites around Rouen, however, and it is near enough to the Le Havre ferry for a
night stop to be organized either coming or going.

If you are travelling between Rouen and Le Havre around September at the
time of equinoctial springs you may be able to see the tidal phenomenon in the
River Seine known as the Mascaret. A wave height of 6 m can occur at Caudebec
if there is a westerly wind. If you take the winding road alongside the Seine you will
find it quite suitable for caravans with a number of convenient stopping-places by the
river.

There is much to see in Normandie that the touring caravanner passes by, not least the beautiful cliffs and beaches of Seine-Maritime, the sands of the Côte Fleurie.

Historic streets unsuitable for caravans . . . Rouen

BRETAGNE

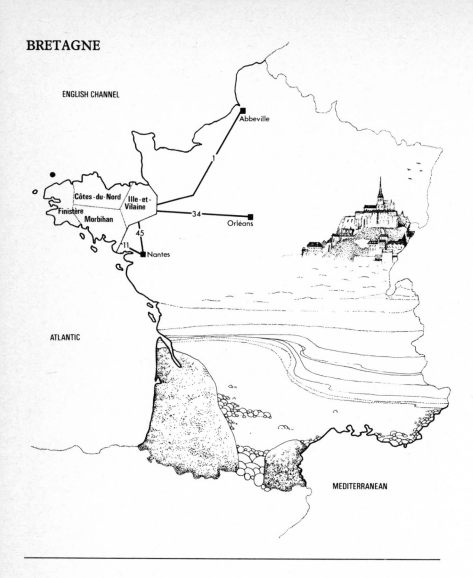

ENGLISH CHANNEL

Abbeville

1

Côtes-du-Nord

Ille-et-Vilaine

Finistère

Morbihan

34

Orléans

45

11

Nantes

ATLANTIC

MEDITERRANEAN

BRETAGNE

Approximate number of camping sites 300

Post no.	Département	Capital
29	Finistère	Quimper
22	Côtes-du-Nord	St. Brieuc
35	Ille-et-Vilaine	Rennes
56	Morbihan	Vannes

Routes connecting 1, 11, 34, 45

One of the most beautiful provinces in France with a great variety of camping sites, many of them around the coastline.

The Emerald Coast (Côte d'Emeraude), extends from the beaches of Mont-St.-Michel to the rocks of Cap Fréhel; from the ***Relaxe site at St. Briac or the ***Longchamp site at St. Lunaire you can enjoy nearby sands and sea and rocks, the rampart-surrounded harbour of St. Malo and the beautiful River Rance leading up to Dinan between steep rocks and cliffs crowned with castles and lined with picturesque villages. There are boat trips from St. Malo or Dinard up the River Rance to Dinan. The navigable channel continues on past Dinan and you will probably see yachts cruising this way to avoid what can be a rough passage around the corner of Finistère. The Canal d'Ille et Rance runs from Dinan to Rennes and the River Vilaine from there to Redon, after which there is a choice of routes to the sea.

Dinard has been called the 'Queen of the Beaches' and it is certainly an elegant resort of rose gardens, mimosa and camellias. Inland is the beautiful castle of Fougères and the castle of Combourg.

The Bay of Granville, Mont-St.-Michel and St. Malo-Dinard claim to have the highest tides in the world; the best time to see them at their most spectacular is in spring and autumn.

The Baie de St. Brieuc and the Côte de Granit Rose make up the rest of the Côtes du Nord, with camping sites all along the coast and the beautiful ****Le Port site at Pleumeur-Bodon, just inland, well situated for exploring coast and country; there are many beaches, some sand, some shingle, with coves and rocks.

Finistère, the French 'Land's End' and most westerly département in France, has a great variety of sites with sand and tide, grass and woods and rocky inlets. Bathing is not always safe.

The principal towns are Brest, Morlaix and Quimper. From Quimper there are boat trips through the gorges of the River Odet to Bénodet.

There are fine sandy beaches all down the Atlantic coast of Morbihan, at Penestin,

Damgan, St. Gildas-de-Rhuys, Port-Navalo, Locmariaquer, La Trinité-sur-Mer, Carnac, Quiberon, Erdeven, Port-Louis, Larmor-Plage and the beaches of Lorient, all with nearby sites.

Pleasure boat trips run regularly from Vannes to the Île-aux-Moines, Port-Navalo, Locmariaquer and the picturesque river of Auray; also more ambitious trips to the islands of Groix, Belle-Île, Houat and Hoëdic; but be warned: the sea in these parts can be rough indeed and the description of Brittany's sea-battered coasts is no exaggeration.

The 'Queen of the Beaches' . . . Dinard

Carnac is a convenient spot from which to explore the magic of Morbihan. There must be almost twenty camping sites in Carnac alone with the ****La Grande Métairie rated the best. It is a little way inland and at the centre of an immense area of megaliths, lined up in rows like a caravan site, which are scattered over fifteen miles of coast. If you wonder at these megaliths you may be interested to know that a menhir is a stone standing vertically on its end; a lech is a menhir which has been hewn and polished by human hands; a dolmen is a flat stone resting horizontally on two or more vertical stones; a gallery grave, a series of dolmens placed end to end; and a cromlech consists of a series of menhirs placed at intervals round the circumference of a circle. At Le Ménec the alignments comprise 1,099 stones in twelve lines, each over a quarter of a mile in length; at Kermario 999 and at Kerlescan 579. At Locmariaquer a gigantic menhir was struck by lightning and now lies in four pieces, the largest of which measures forty feet long. Originally it measured only ten feet less than the obelisk in the Place de la Concorde in Paris. Alongside is the dolmen, or 'Merchants' Table', weighing approximately one hundred tons. Imagine prehistoric people lifting, carrying and erecting such prodigious masses!

Stretching out to the sea from near Carnac is the Quiberon peninsula. Quiberon was once an island, but is now attached to the mainland by a narrow isthmus of sand. Amongst the sand-dunes and pines there are half a dozen camping sites and the holiday resort of Quiberon.

There is never enough time in Brittany; your plans are continually being altered because you are sidetracked by beauty and interest everywhere competing for your attention and enjoyment. Throughout the summer there are numerous festivals and in many places you see the traditional costume with its lace head-dress worn by the Breton womenfolk, particularly in Lower Brittany.

If you love caravanning in France you will be captivated by Brittany.

VAL DE LOIRE

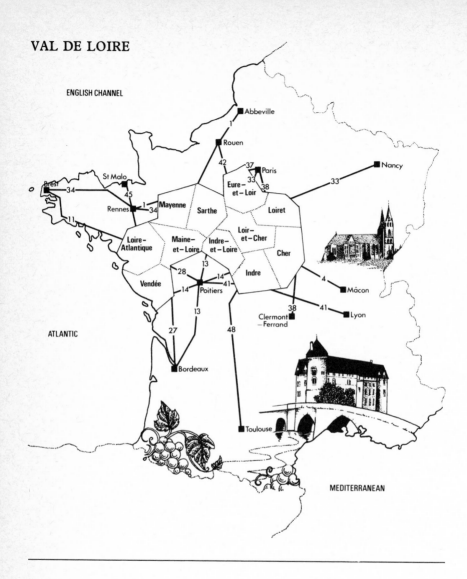

ENGLISH CHANNEL

Abbeville

1

Rouen

42

37
33
Paris

Eure—
et — Loir

38

33

Nancy

St Malo

0
Brest
34

45

1
Rennes
34
Mayenne

Sarthe

Loiret

11

Loire—
Atlantique

Maine—
et — Loire

Indre—
et — Loire

Loir—
et — Cher

Cher

4
Mâcon

28

13

14
41

Indre

Vendée

14
Poitiers

41
Lyon

13

38
Clermont
—Ferrand

ATLANTIC

27

48

Bordeaux

Toulouse

MEDITERRANEAN

VAL DE LOIRE

Approximate number of camping sites   600

Post no.	Département	Capital
53	Mayenne	Laval
72	Sarthe	Le Mans
44	Loire-Atlantique	Nantes
49	Maine-et-Loire	Angers
85	Vendée	La Roche-s-Yon
28	Eure-et-Loir	Chartres
45	Loiret	Orléans
41	Loir-et-Cher	Blois
37	Indre-et-Loire	Tours
36	Indre	Châteauroux
18	Cher	Bourges

Routes connecting   1, 2, 3, 4, 11, 13, 14, 27, 28, 29, 33, 34, 37, 38, 41, 42, 45, 48

The main concentration of camping sites is on the Atlantic coast of Vendée and Loire-Atlantique and along the banks of the rivers Loire, Mayenne, Sarthe, Loir, Vienne, Indre, Cher and Sauldre.

Route No. 3 will take you to Les Sables d'Olonne, a most attractive holiday resort with many camping sites to the right and left of it; in fact there are over a hundred and seventy sites on this stretch of coast, by which you can judge its popularity.

Several routes lead to Nantes, from which it is a short drive to a good selection of coastal sites on either side of the Loire estuary.

It is claimed that this coastline of Vendée and Loire-Atlantique enjoys as much light and sunshine as the Riviera; the proximity of the Gulf Stream contributes to a unique climate and the bracing air is said to be laden with iodine and ultra-violet rays. The resorts of this coast, with their promenades and flowers and gay beach umbrellas splashing colour along the sand and shore are every bit as attractive as the better-known seaside towns of the Mediterranean.

Apart from the fact that this beautiful coast is probably 200 km. nearer to the Channel ports than the Mediterranean, there is another holiday advantage in directing your caravan tour this way; you will be able to see some of the châteaux of the Loire. The great châteaux are situated on, or near to, the Loire extending from Angers to Orléans, and in this area there are over a hundred camping sites, many delightful quite apart from their proximity to so much beauty and historic interest.

Chambord, largest of the Châteaux of the Loire

To appreciate all the historic attractions of this area it is advisable to have the Michelin Guide (printed in English), *Châteaux of the Loire.*

Before planning a tour of the château area it is also worthwhile to ascertain when and where the Son et Lumière (sound and light), spectacles are being held. Obviously these take place at night, but you can pick a camping site near to the son et lumière display that you wish to see so that you need not worry about keeping children out of bed longer than necessary. These displays, in such fairy-tale settings, with the magic of colour, floodlit and with the drama of sound, take you right back into history in the most impressive fashion. Even if you are accustomed to regarding history and monuments as a bore you cannot fail to be stirred. But you will be compelled to take an interest in history here for the château spectacles are unique in the world.

From Tours along the River Cher towards Bourges there are also many beautiful sites and around Tours are grouped the Châteaux of Touraine.

There is a noted château in Nantes too, and various other attractions, for instance the port and the nearby resorts.

The other rivers in the Val de Loire are equally beautiful, with sufficient sites spaced out along their banks.

The peak time for caravan holidays in this province is the same as for the rest of France: mid-July to the end of August, although the sites along the Sarthe around Le Mans sometimes get crowded in June at the time of the motor race.

POITOU-CHARENTES

Approximate number of camping sites 150

Post no.	Département	Capital
86	Vienne	Poitiers
79	Deux-Sèvres	Niort
17	Charente-Maritime	La Rochelle
16	Charente	Angoulême

Routes connecting 5, 13, 14, 27, 28, 41

A fair number of British caravanners have realized the attractions of this coast; those who stick to the Mediterranean cannot somehow believe that the French Atlantic resorts are as attractive as the resorts of the French Mediterranean.

Of the four départements of Poitou-Charentes only one, Charente-Maritime, is on the sea. The principal resorts are Royan and La Rochelle, although this latter town is probably more a commercial and fishing port than a resort in the accepted sense. There is a beach with a beautiful park adjacent at La Rochelle and, of course, the harbour with its towers is fascinating, as is the town.

There are camping sites at La Rochelle and nearby, but you see the greatest number of caravans on the off-lying Île de Ré. On the coast down to Royan and below there is also a good selection of sites with many on the Île d'Oléron; you can take your caravan across to this 'island' quite easily on the toll road. Oléron is twenty miles long by four wide, a pleasant place of sand dunes, beaches, pine woods and probably more than thirty sites.

Royan is an important resort with many hotels and fine beaches. There are half a dozen sites here and it is a convenient centre from which to explore. You can cross to the Médoc peninsula from here on the car ferry.

Away from the coast there are castles and churches of historic interest, particularly between Angoulême and Poitiers. The name of Poitiers lingers with schoolday memories of the prowess of English archers here. There is a splendid open market at Poitiers and it is a most attractive little town.

Just below Poitiers there is a pleasant site at Lusignan, the **de Vauchiron; this is almost equidistant between Poitiers and Niort. Near Niort there is a quaint area of canals on which you can take boat trips round the fields and under the trees.

Further south at Angoulême you can look out from the ramparts over the Charente valley. The ***BOURGINES site is a convenient centre from which to explore the varied features of the area. Members of the party not interested in history may find a visit to nearby Cognac more to their liking; the vaults of Martell, Hennessy

POITOU – CHARENTES

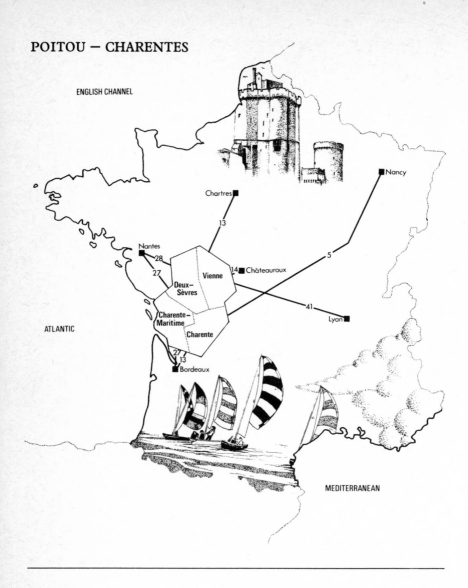

ENGLISH CHANNEL

Nancy

Chartres

13

Nantes
28
27

Vienne

14 Châteauroux

5

Deux–
Sèvres

41 Lyon

Charente–
Maritime

ATLANTIC

Charente

27
13

Bordeaux

MEDITERRANEAN

The Atlantic resorts are also attractive . . . Royan

and Otard are open to visitors. Next to the French, the British are apparently the biggest brandy-drinking nation, so that you can be sure of a welcome.

If you are returning from Cognac to Royan you will pass through Saintes on the River Charente. This is a remarkable old Roman city with a triumphal arch and other Roman remains.

LIMOUSIN

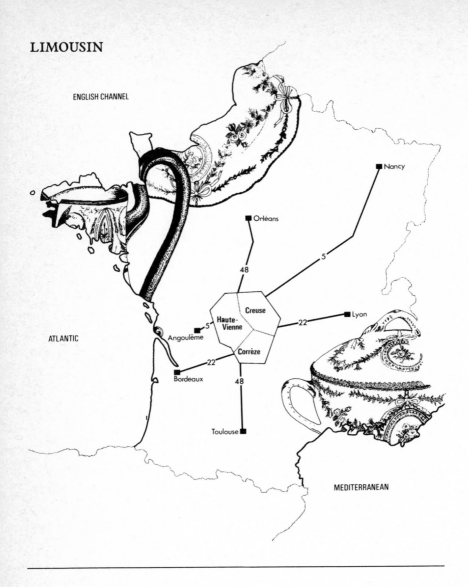

ENGLISH CHANNEL

Nancy

ATLANTIC

Orléans

48

5

Creuse

Haute-Vienne

5

Angoulême

22

Lyon

Corrèze

22

Bordeaux

48

Toulouse

MEDITERRANEAN

LIMOUSIN

Approximate number of camping sites   80

Post no.	Département	Capital
23	Creuse	Guéret
87	Haute-Vienne	Limoges
19	Corrèze	Tulle

Routes connecting   5, 22, 48

The ****MUNICIPAL camping site is very pleasantly situated on the River Vienne at Limoges. The town is not really in a central position for exploring Limousin but it does possess the largest museum in the world devoted to porcelain and ceramics, the Adrien Dubouché National Museum; there are displayed ten thousand remarkable pieces representing all periods and gathered from all countries. The Municipal Museum also displays regional enamels from the twelfth century to the present time in a collection of over 300 enamels. Limoges is the world capital of ceramic and allied arts and if these are your interests you should certainly stop at the ****MUNICIPAL site here.

Limoges is the regional capital of the Limousin and in this part of Haute-Vienne there are some very pleasant camping sites, including the ****Leychoisier site at Bonnac-la-Côte and the ****Beaufort site at St. Léonard-de-Noblat, that are equal to the ****MUNICIPAL site at Limoges.

The part of Haute-Vienne around Limoges and the département of Corrèze is the former countship of Limousin. Caravan sites are more in evidence here and along the River Dordogne where it forms the border of Corrèze than elsewhere in Limousin.

When you think of Limousin you think of the Massif Central, the north-western part of which is in the département of Creuse and partly in Haute-Vienne; understandably there are not a great many sites in this area, which rises to over 3,000 ft. in places. Although described as 'pretty hill country' there are many less arduous areas for a caravan to explore.

In the Dordogne valley are many attractive sites. At Bort les Orgues, on the River Dordogne near the confluence of the River Rhue, are huge volcanic 'organ pipes' which have given the town its name. Nearby, the beautiful Château de Val rises out of the huge artificial lake of Bort. It is in a beautiful and unspoilt corner of the upper Dordogne where there are two world-famous spas. The **MUNICIPAL camping site is within two hundred yards of the River Dordogne.

AQUITAINE

Approximate number of camping sites   340

Post no.	Département	Capital
24	Dordogne	Périgueux
33	Gironde	Bordeaux
47	Lot-et-Garonne	Agen
40	Landes	Mont-de-Marsan
64	Pyrénées-Atlantique *or* Basses-Pyrénées	Pau

Routes connecting   8, 9, 10, 13, 22, 27, 28, 35

For the caravanner this province has everything: sea, beaches, resorts, the Basque
country, forests, mountains, rivers, splendid towns and wine.

Biarritz is known as the Jewel of the Basque Coast and is the principal resort of
the province, deservedly so for it is one of the most celebrated resorts in some of
the most beautiful surroundings in the world.

There are pleasant camping sites in Biarritz, also along the coast on either side;
probably ten sites at Bidart, a dozen each at St.-Jean-de-Luz and Hendaye by the
Spanish border. If you have stowed surf-boards in your caravan you will be able to
use them here.

It is preferable to establish a base, say at the ***La Chambre d'Amour site (the
name is a promising start to a holiday), at Anglet or at one of the Biarritz sites and
to explore the Pyrénées by car without the caravan in tow. At Pau you will be able
to see the view from the Boulevard des Pyrénées.

There are camping sites throughout Pyrénées-Atlantique if you would rather
bring your caravan along with you.

Above Biarritz and the Basque Country is the département of Landes, a strangely
deserted area, considering its location, of forests and sandy plains. There are
camping sites all the way up the coastline of Landes and also around the two lakes,
the Étang de Cazaux and the Étang de Biscarrosse.

Just above, in the Gironde, is Arcachon with the highest sand dunes in Europe
(the Dune of Pylat is 350 ft. high). Arcachon is a fine holiday resort on the shores
of a land-locked bay, the Bassin d'Arcachon, eight miles wide and ideal for water
sports. Around the bay are thirty or more caravan sites and the situation has everything for a successful holiday: the sea with good surfing, beautiful sands, a fishing
harbour and nearby Bordeaux.

Bordeaux has the advantage of being an interesting city and yet not a tourist
centre. The Bordeaux vineyards produce some of the finest wines in the world,
half in red and half in white.

The red wines are: Médoc, Graves, St.-Emilion, Pomerol, Côtes de Fronsac,

AQUITAINE

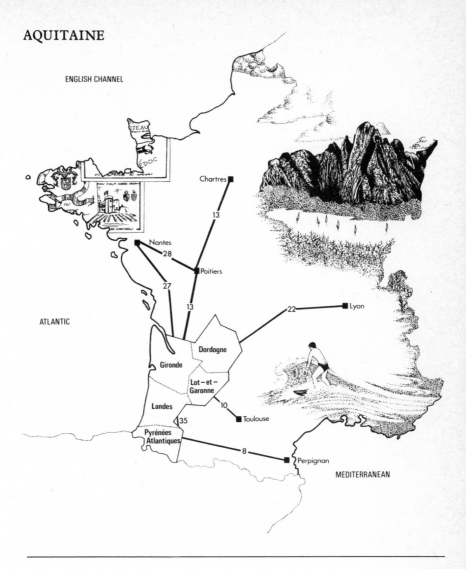

ENGLISH CHANNEL

Chartres

13

Nantes

28

Poitiers

27

13

ATLANTIC

22 Lyon

Dordogne

Gironde

Lot – et –
Garonne

Landes

10

Toulouse

35

Pyrénées
Atlantiques

8

Perpignan

MEDITERRANEAN

Côtes de Bourg et de Blaye and Entre-deux-Mers.

The Médoc is the triangle between the Atlantic and the rivers Garonne and Gironde; there are produced Saint-Estèphe, Pauillac, Saint-Julien, Listrac, Moulis and Margaux. The region extending from the Médoc to the south-west of Bordeaux is the Graves de Bordeaux.

The picturesque village of St.-Emilion has a number of communes nearby including Montagne, Lussac, Puisseguin, Saint-Georges, Parsac and Sables.

The white wines extend from Entre-deux-Mers and of the region of Blaye to the great wines of Sauternes and Cérons with the white Graves wines and also

There are many sites near St. Jean de Luz

the famous white wines of the right bank of the Garonne coming from the Premières Côtes de Bordeaux, Langoiran, Cadillac, Loupiac and Sainte-Croix-du-Mont. The Syndicat d'Initiative in Bordeaux will be pleased to arrange visits to vineyards and wine caves. Combining wine with castles you could see: Château Margaux, (1er Cru Classé A Margaux), Château Guiraud, (1er Cru Classé Sauternes), Château d'Yquem, (Grand Premier Cru du Sauternes), Château Latour, (1er Cru Classé Pauillac).

Just inland from Bordeaux is the region of Périgord and the Dordogne.

The ***BARNABE-PLAGE site by the River Isle at Périgueux is a convenient centre from which to explore. It is an area noted for prehistoric art, wooded valleys, fortified châteaux and Roman remains.

As a centre for the most complete caravan holiday Aquitaine has everything you could wish for.

PYRÉNÉES

Approximate number of camping sites 300

Post no.	Département	Capital
46	Lot	Cahors
12	Aveyron	Rodez
82	Tarn-et-Garonne	Montauban
32	Gers	Auch
31	Haute-Garonne	Toulouse
81	Tarn	Albi
65	Hautes-Pyrénées	Tarbes
09	Ariège	Foix

Routes connecting   8, 10, 25, 34, 46, 47, 48, 49

In this large area in the south-western corner of France, between the Atlantic and the Mediterranean with the Pyrénées/Spanish border as a base, the greatest number of camping sites is in the south of the province in the département of Hautes-Pyrénées.

The scenery in the Pyrénées is breathtaking, but some of the roads are twisting and difficult; yet if you have ambitions to explore the high altitudes you can take comfort from the fact that thousands of caravanners journey to the mountain sites every year. But – and this is all-important – they pick their road. If you study your map you will be surprised to find how often there are alternatives to the worst sections in the Pyrénées; obviously you should plan your route before you set off.

A compromise is to leave your caravan on, say, one of the dozen sites at Lourdes and take the car only to explore the Pyrénées. Whilst at Lourdes you might be glad of the opportunity to be present at one of the great torchlight processions.

Climbing 30 km. south from Lourdes you come to Cauterets, a popular winter and summer resort and spa. Over 3,000 ft. up, Cauterets is situated on Lac de Gaube. There is another lake, Lac d'Oredon, adjoining, and a famous bridge, the Pont d'Espagne, with spectacular scenery all around. There are half a dozen camping sites at Cauterets and many others in these high regions and leading up to them. Many caravanners are understandably reluctant to haul their outfits up steep roads and round hairpin beds, but it is a rewarding and satisfying experience when you back your caravan on to a pitch that seems to be on the roof of the world.

Moving up north from Lourdes, past Tarbes and into the département of Gers you will find the ★★★MUNICIPAL site at Auch a pleasant centre from which to explore the centre of what was once Gascony.

The bright pink buildings of Toulouse are also worth a visit; there are many Renaissance buildings in this attractive town and the ★★★MUNICIPAL site is conveniently situated by the Pont du Rupé.

PYRÉNÉES

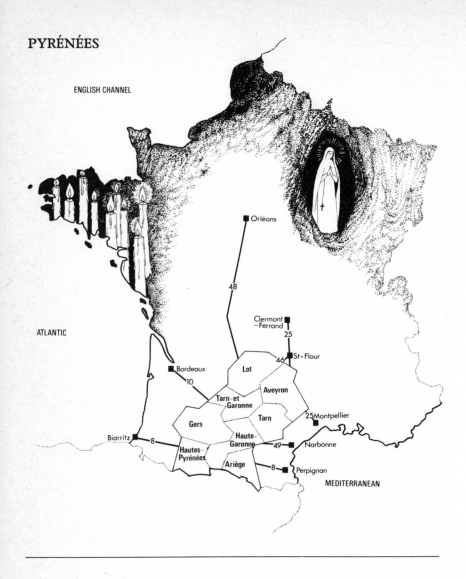

ENGLISH CHANNEL

ATLANTIC

■ Orléans

48

Clermont
—Ferrand ■
25
46 ■ St-Flour

■ Bordeaux   Lot
10
Aveyron
Tarn-et-
Garonne
25 Montpellier
Gers   Tarn
Biarritz ■   Haute-
8   Garonne   49 ■
Hautes-   ■ Narbonne
Pyrénées
Ariège   8 ■ Perpignan

MEDITERRANEAN

An ancient province between Périgord and Rouergue, the region known as Quercy corresponds to the département of Lot and here in Quercy prehistory has left unique wall drawings. The ★★★Les Pins site at Payrac is conveniently nearby; also near is the Gouffre de Padirac, a river 300 ft. below ground. It has been open to visitors since 1898 and is still claimed to be the greatest of all caves and potholes discovered in the last century. This is no ordinary pothole, for you go down in one of four lifts and below there are two river craft to take you on a cruise of the subterranean river.

Going from the depths to the heights it is not really very far across to the Causse de Sauveterre and the Causse Méjean in Aveyron, a chasm over thirty miles long and over 1,500 ft. deep in places. A good site from which to view the Gorges du Tarn would be the ***Rêve du Pêcheur lakeside camping site at Notre-Dame d'Aures, or perhaps the ****Municipal site at Millau.

If your idea of a caravan holiday is to see some of the wonderful works of nature then the province of Pyrénées is for you.

The largest church in France . . . Toulouse

CHAMPAGNE

Approximate number of camping sites 65

Post no.	Département	Capital
08	Ardennes	Mézières
51	Marne	Châlons-sur-Marne
10	Aube	Troyes
52	Haute-Marne	Chaumont

Routes connecting   5, 7, 18, 21, 33, 39, 40, 44

Much of the province is flat but there are hills and valleys here and there, also the forests of Argonne, Ardennes, Aube and Haute-Marne. The disposition of camping sites is adequate but they are not numerous.

Situated between the Île de France and Lorraine, with Belgium to the north and Burgundy to the south, Champagne has cathedrals and First World War battlefields to see as well as vineyards; but most caravanners who pause here, say at the ***Camp du Champagne at Reims, bring back memories of Pommery and Greno's eleven-mile underground cellar there or of the wine cellars of Mumm, Taittinger or Pommery, or of Moët et Chandon's cellars at Épernay. In Piper Heidsieck's cellars you tour by underground train. Whilst in Reims you should, of course, visit the magnificent Gothic cathedral where most of the kings of France were crowned.

Another pleasant little centre from which to explore the mysteries of Champagne is the ***Municipal site at Épernay on the River Marne. The town itself is charming, with delightful public gardens. Underneath it, dug out of the chalk, there are enormous galleries containing millions of bottles. You can visit the Museum of Champagne in the Château in Avenue de Champagne.

Thousands of visitors go either to Reims or to Épernay to watch the champagne being made.

There are three routes or circuits through the vineyards, each circuit being indicated in the appropriate colour. The Green Circuit starts from Épernay and runs round the Côtes des Blancs, D.40 and D.10. The Red Circuit runs from Ay to Châtillon-sur-Marne, the valley of the Marne via Hautvilliers. The Blue Circuit starts from Reims and takes in the Montagne de Reims area.

Near to Épernay is Dormans, a small market town with a memorial of the First World War, la Chapelle de la Marne, but the principal war memorials are near Verdun. The road from Bar-le-Duc to Verdun is known as the Voie Sacrée, the Sacred Way, crossing the battlefields. At Verdun there are two 'Tours of the Battlefields of the First World War', one on the right bank, the Circuit des Forts, and one

CHAMPAGNE

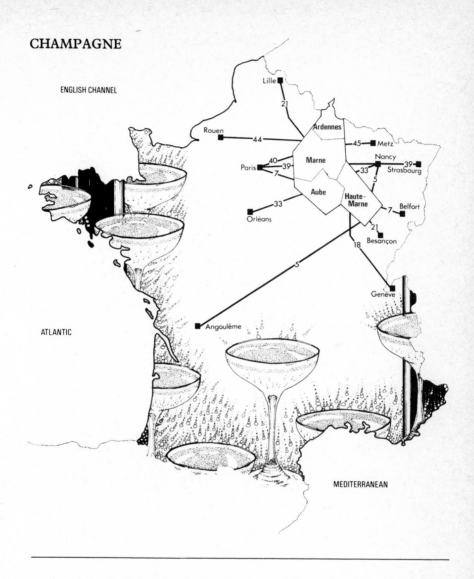

ENGLISH CHANNEL

ATLANTIC

MEDITERRANEAN

Lille

Rouen   44

Paris   40
         39
         7

Ardennes

Metz   45

Marne

Nancy
         39
Strasbourg
         33
         5

Aube

Haute-
Marne
         7   Belfort

Orléans   33

         21
Besançon

         18

         5

Genève

Angoulême

on the left bank of the Meuse. A convenient small camping site near Verdun is the **Sous le Moulin at Charny-sur-Meuse, a little way back from the main road traffic.

There is certainly a lot of traffic in the province of Champagne and you get the impression that every main road going anywhere passes through it; it is, in fact, on the way from the north to the Alps and to the Mediterranean and from Paris to the eastern industrial zone.

In the north of the province is the Ardennes, adjoining Luxembourg and Belgium. The capital, Mézières (sometimes called Charleville-Mézières, but Charleville is

Twelfth-century St. Urbain church at Troyes

on one side of the Meuse and Mézières is on the other), is an attractive town with a Place Ducale. The ★★★Mont-Olympe site is on the river.

The forest of Ardennes is certainly a place in which to get away from it all, interesting and gloomy in parts, but relieved by the beautiful valley of the Meuse. A convenient centre from which to explore is Revin, a charming little town. Pleasant sites in the area are the ★★Rocher de l'Uf at Fumay and the ★★Moraypré at Haybes.

If you are in Champagne in the autumn you should hasten to the wine roads for the joy of driving through miles of the golden harvest of the vineyards.

ALSACE

Approximate number of camping sites   100

Post no.	Département	Capital
67	Bas-Rhin	Strasbourg
68	Haut-Rhin	Colmar

Routes connecting   39

You rarely see caravans with GB plates in this corner of France. It is not that caravanners are unadventurous, for you see them in many unexpected places; perhaps in planning and consulting maps they are put off by the proximity of the Saar or by the industrial-sounding names of some of the towns.

The place names in Alsace are mostly German because of its German background, history and culture. Alsace has see-sawed between French and German rule (not counting the Second World War), having reverted to France after the First War and having been German since the Franco-Prussian war of 1871 – perhaps it is sufficient to say that it has had a colourful history. You will see that the towns and villages and buildings generally are 'German style' and the language, or Alsatian dialect, is basically German although the official language is French.

Another possible reason for the reluctance of some caravanners to explore this province is the presence of the Vosges mountains. Route 39 through Nancy and Strasbourg passes through Sarrebourg (800 ft., Moselle, Lorraine), and Saverne (650 ft., Bas-Rhin, Alsace) and barely ten miles of beautiful area south the boundary between Alsace and Lorraine is at an altitude of over 2,000 ft.

There is not a large selection of camping sites in this northern area nor across towards the Rhine at the border. The Rhine and the Canal du Rhône au Rhin here seem to be too busily concerned with their commerce and river traffic to bother about anything else.

In the Central Vosges area just below Strasbourg there are not many sites but the nearby ***MUNICIPAL site at Obernai is a pleasant centre from which to explore the beautiful mountain regions and resorts nearby.

Coming south into Haut-Rhin the ***PIERRE DE COUBERTIN site at Ribeauvillé and the ****INTERCOMMUNAL site at Riquewihr are in the vineyard country and most of the camping sites in the province are in this region. Riquewihr is an old wine town said to be the most picturesque in Alsace and is well worth a visit. Only five miles away is Aubure, at 2,500 ft. the highest village in Alsace.

ALSACE

There are many ancient wine towns, castles and timber houses. At Ribeauvillé alone there are three ruined castles and here are produced those wonderful Alsatian wines, Riesling and Traminer. If you are here during the annual festival in September you will be able to enjoy music and dancing and FREE WINE!

During the summer the principal towns along what is called the Wine Road of Alsace are all floodlit.

Alsace is a beautiful and exciting province in which to spend a caravan holiday, particularly in Haut-Rhin whose capital, Colmar, is a most picturesque town of painted houses with many treasures of art and architecture.

96

'German style' building . . . Colmar

LORRAINE

Approximate number of camping sites 100

Post no.	Département	Capital
55	Meuse	Bar-le-Duc
57	Moselle	Metz
54	Meurthe-et-Moselle	Nancy
88	Vosges	Epinal

Routes connecting 5, 26, 33, 39, 40

There is a lot of industry in Lorraine, particularly between Nancy and Luxembourg, in the middle of which is Metz which sounds industrial and is. Metz is rarely included in the itinerary of caravanners but, although industrial, it is agreeably situated on the rivers Seille and Moselle. Once an important Roman city and once centre of the Carolingian Empire, Metz has a number of interesting buildings and churches including St. Étienne cathedral which has been described as a masterpiece of Gothic art.

There is also a lot of history in Lorraine; the more recent history of the First War is brought to the minds of older visitors by the mention of Verdun. Many monuments and cemeteries recall this.

But Lorraine has a principal claim to fame as the birth-place of the patron saint of France, Joan of Arc. It is interesting to visit her birth-place and the countryside where she lived as a child because they are still much the same as they were in her time.

The ***BRABOIS camping site, just south of Nancy on the N.74, is a convenient place from which to visit Joan's birthplace at Domrémy. The house where she was born may be seen and nearby is a museum. A son et lumière display is presented at Domrémy in the summer. In the woods at Bois-Chenu she first heard the voices calling her to liberate France. At Vaucouleurs Joan asked the Governor, Robert de Baudricourt, for an escort to take her to Charles VII. The ruins of Château de Baudricourt may be visited.

The rest of the history of Joan of Arc lies outside Lorraine. See:

Route 4: Chinon, Château de Coudray, where Joan saw Charles VII.

Route 33: Orléans, where the Maid of Orléans drove off the English invaders, 8 May 1429.

Route 21: Reims, where Joan was present at the coronation of Charles VII on 17 July 1429.

LORRAINE

Route 44: Compiègne, where Joan was captured by the Burgundians and handed over to the English, 1430.

Route 1: Rouen, where Joan or Arc was burnt at the stake by the English on 30 May 1431.

Apart from industry Lorraine is made up of agricultural land and forests and includes the areas of the upper Meuse and the upper Moselle. Camping sites are

La Pucelle d'Orléans (the Maid of Orleans); monument at Domrémy-la-Pucelle

comparatively thinly spread throughout the upper départements which, in a way, suffer from having attractive neighbours, Champagne on the one side and the Vosges on the other, with the Ardennes above. The southern département of Vosges is well served with attractive sites.

BOURGOGNE

Approximate number of camping sites 100

Post no.	Département	Capital
89	Yonne	Auxerre
21	Côte-d'Or	Dijon
58	Nièvre	Nevers
71	Saône-et-Loire	Mâcon

Routes connecting   4, 5, 12, 18, 33, 36, 38

Bourgogne, or Burgundy, is, of course, the province of wine, of beautiful country and vineyards.

It is likely that most caravanners who have been to the Mediterranean have passed through part of Bourgogne, for the A.6 autoroute runs through Yonne not a 100 km. from Paris and on through the Côte d'Or.

The principal vineyards of the Côte d'Or lie between Dijon and Chalon-sur-Saône, a small area compared to the Mâconnais and Chalonnais and the Beaujolais region below, whose wines do not enjoy the distinction of those of the Côte d'Or. Chablis, above, borders the autoroute, level with Auxerre.

There are over a hundred Appellations Contrôlées in Burgundy. Practically every inch of land of the Côte d'Or is given over to the vine, but enough has been spared at Meursault for a pleasant camping site, the ***La Grappe d'Or and the ***Les Cent Vignes at Beaune.

The Syndicat d'Initiative office in Beaune will be pleased to give you details of visits to the wine cellars and wine tastings.

Since the names of the vineyards read like a wine list you will no doubt recognize many place names of the Côte d'Or, some of which are:

In the Côte de Beaune – Santenay, Chassagne-Montrachet, Puligny-Montrachet, Meursault, Volnay, Pommard, Beaune, Aloxe-Corton.

In the Côte de Nuits – Nuits-St.-Georges, Vosne-Romanée, Vougeot, Chambolle-Musigny, Morey-St.-Denis, Gevrey-Chambertin.

Apart from the wine, Bourgogne is a most pleasant place of rivers and small lakes, forests and open country. There are châteaux at Châteauneuf, Ancy-le-France, Bussy-Rabutin, La Rochepot and Vougeot, Burgundian abbeys at Auxerre, Tournus, Dijon, Vézelay, Cluny, Citeaux, Fontenay and La Charité-sur-Loire.

Camping sites are well spread throughout the province and many are in attractive situations: by lakes, de Chaumeçon and des Settons, and by rivers and canals, the Loire and Saône.

On the canals du Nivernais and du Bourgogne you may sometimes see yachts

BOURGOGNE

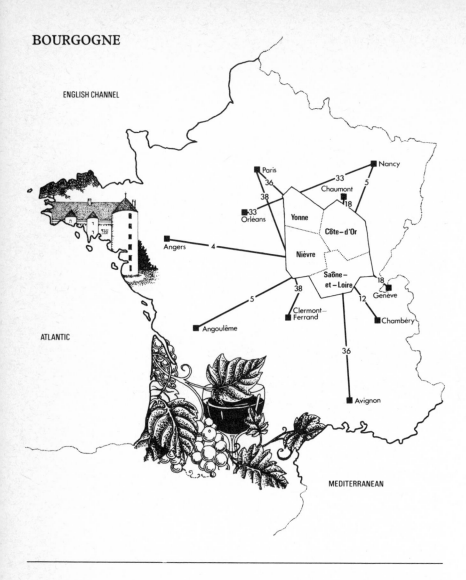

ENGLISH CHANNEL

ATLANTIC

Paris

Nancy

36
33
Chaumont
5
38
18
Orléans 33
Yonne
Côte–d'Or
Angers 4
Nièvre
Saône–
et–Loire
18
38
Genève
5
12
Clermont—
Ferrand
Chambéry
Angoulême
36
Avignon

MEDITERRANEAN

cruising along as a change from the picturesque barge traffic. These canals are the inland waterway routes through France from the Channel to the Mediterranean.

If you are likely to take your caravan to the Mediterranean it is also likely that you will make a night stop in or near Bourgogne; if you decide to pause for a time to explore the beauty of this province you will probably want to stay.

The signposts read like a wine list

AUVERGNE

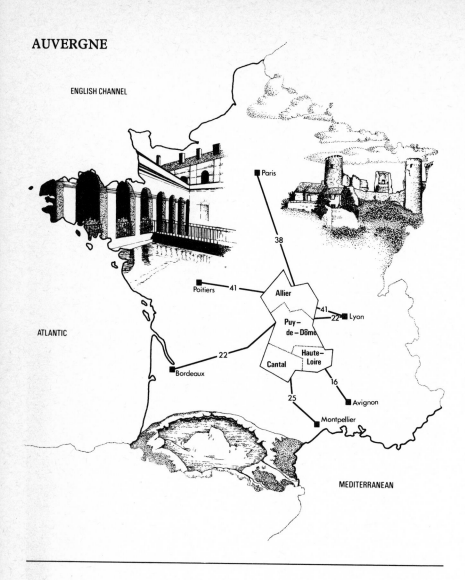

ENGLISH CHANNEL

Paris

38

ATLANTIC

Poitiers 41

Allier

41 22 Lyon

Puy – de – Dôme

22

Haute– Loire

Cantal

Bordeaux

16

25 Avignon

Montpellier

MEDITERRANEAN

AUVERGNE

Approximate number of camping sites   150

Post no.	Département	Capital
03	Allier	Moulins
63	Puy-de-Dôme	Clermont-Ferrand
15	Cantal	Aurillac
43	Haute-Loire	Le Puy

Routes connecting   1, 5, 16, 22, 25, 38, 41, 46

Auvergne is in the centre of France, a province of mountains and extinct volcanoes, one of the most curious regions in Europe. Some craters have become lakes, for instance the almost circular Lac Pavin, a strange place surrounded by brooding forests. Elsewhere a lava flow has dammed a small stream which has thus become lakes such as Lac Chambon, Lac d'Aydat and many others.

From the semi-molten interior gush thermal springs, all that remains of volcanic activity, with sufficient healing properties to attract thousands.

These mineral springs were appreciated by the Romans and today the modern health resorts of Vichy, Châtel-Guyon, Royat, Le Mont-Doré and La Bourboule are equipped with every amenity.

Caravanners seeking the cure (for digestive troubles mainly), will find themselves well catered for with sites. There are four shown at Vichy in ROUTE 38, the ***Clos de Balanède at Chatel-Guyon, the *Le Petit Boulogne at Royat, the ***Les Crouzets at Le Mont-Doré and the ***Les Vernières and **Poutié at La Bourboule. On a more modest curative level you may be satisfied with a bottle of Vichy water which you will have no difficulty in obtaining, for the famous Source des Célestins produces nearly 50,000 gallons a day.

Caravanners attracted to the mountains may be interested to learn that the camping site at the highest altitude is the **les Sapins at La Chaise-Dieu (3,550 ft.), followed by the ***Les Crouzets site already mentioned at Le Mont-Doré (3,450 ft.) and the ****Municipal site at Sauges (3,150 ft.). What have they to offer the caravanner?

La Chaisse-Dieu is on a high plateau of pasture land and fir trees and is mainly renowned for its fourteenth-century abbey with its famous tempera painting of the Danse Macabre in the north aisle, six feet high and eighty-five feet long. There is also the tomb of Pope Clement VI. At nearby Chavaniac is the château where de Lafayette was born in 1757, with a museum containing souvenirs of him and of America's part in the First War.

Le Mont-Doré is in the centre of the highest volcanic chain in Auvergne at the foot of its main summit, the Puy de Sancy, undoubtedly enjoying the finest mountain scenery in the province. Principally a spa as mentioned above, Le Mont-Doré is set amidst pasture lands and pinewoods. It is the nearest winter sports centre to Paris with two cable cars, a funicular, ten drag lifts and forty miles of ski runs.

Sauges is a pleasant summer resort with a trout stream.

There are many camping sites throughout Auvergne and caravanners are attracted by the simpler pleasures of relaxation in pure and healthy surroundings. Auvergne is thinly populated and it is a delight to come across small forgotten villages, deep forests, lakes and waterfalls, all conducive to absolute peace and restfulness.

The health-giving properties of Auvergne are not found only in its spas.

You may seek the cure here . . . La Bourboule

FRANCHE - COMTÉ

Approximate number of camping sites   90

Post no.	Département	Capital
70	Haute-Saône	Vesoul
90	Territoire-de-Belfort	Belfort
25	Doubs	Besançon
39	Jura	Lons-le-Saunier

Routes connecting   7, 18, 21, 26

When you think of Franche-Comté you think of the Juras, trout from the mountain streams, crayfish from the lakes and mushrooms from the woods with Arlay white wine or Arbois straw wine ('the more one drinks the straighter one walks').

Franche-Comté varies in altitude from 1,000 ft. to 5,500 ft., rising in ridges along the borders of Switzerland and along the Jura chain of mountains. It has a great variety of scenery, plains rich with the colour of flowers, dark forests, valleys of the rivers Saône, Ognon and Doubs, deep gorges such as those at Nouailles, broad plateaux culminating in dramatic cliffs as at Cirque de Consolation, Baume-les-Messieurs, pasture land and mountains like Mont d'Or (4,800 ft.), and La Dôle (5,500 ft.).

There are clear springs, the sources of the rivers Loue, Lison and Dessoubre, rivers with stretches of rapids such as the Haut-Doubs and Loue, the Doubs waterfall and the Hérisson cascades, whirlpools, lakes, caves and caverns, views of the whole Alpine chain and over Geneva from the Col de la Faucille (4,336 ft.). But, the caravanner should be warned, there are many hairpin bends.

You will gather that Franche-Comté is a province of mountains and forests, rivers and lakes.

Most of the camping sites are in the southern half of the province, in Doubs and Jura. The ★★★Martinet site at St.-Claude is in a convenient situation for exploring. Although described as an industrial town (manufacturing pipes and inlaid woodwork), St. Claude (1,443 ft.), is famous for its situation at the confluence of the rivers Bienne and Tacon and is the tourist centre of the Haut-Jura. It is noted for its waterfalls, grottoes and gorges.

There are thermal resorts at Besançon, Lons-le-Saunier, Luxeuil-les-Bains and Salins, winter sports resorts at Metabief and Les Rousses, which is only one mile away from Switzerland.

Any caravanner who carries his fishing rod will be interested to learn that there are more fish in the rivers and lakes of Franche-Comté than anywhere in France;

FRANCHE — COMTÉ

ENGLISH CHANNEL

Lille

ATLANTIC

Paris

21

7

Chaumont

Nancy

26

7

Haute–
Saône

Tre–de
Belfort

18

Doubs

Jura

26

Lyon

MEDITERRANEAN

in the Saône, Doubs, Loue, Ognon, Ain and the Lac de Saint-Point with, in addition, innumerable brooks swarming with crayfish.

Franche-Comté is a province in which you will enjoy outdoor activity amidst beautiful scenery.

Deep gorges . . . Cirque des Baumes

VALLÉE DU RHÔNE

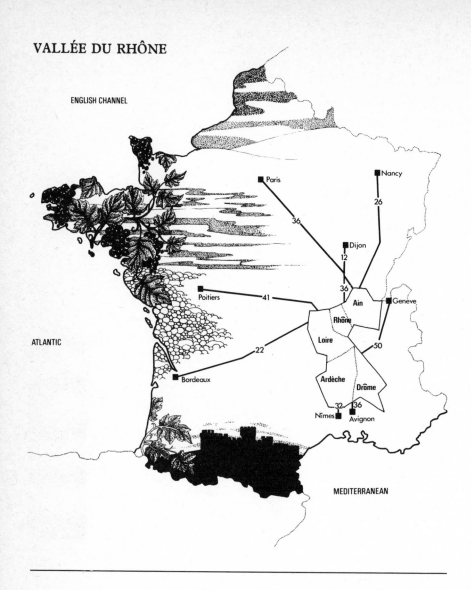

ENGLISH CHANNEL

ATLANTIC

MEDITERRANEAN

Nancy

26

Paris

36

Dijon

12

36

Ain

Genève

Poitiers

41

Rhône

Loire

50

22

Ardèche

Drôme

Bordeaux

32

36

Nîmes

Avignon

VALLÉE DU RHÔNE

Approximate number of camping sites   200

Post no.	Département	Capital
01	Ain	Bourg-en-Bresse
69	Rhône	Lyon
42	Loire	St. Étienne
07	Ardèche	Privas
26	Drôme	Valence

Routes connecting   12, 22, 26, 32, 36, 41, 50

Caravanners who make an early start from their cross-Channel port are usually nearing the Rhône valley on the second day and by then the strain of the journey gives way to excitement as the nearness of the Mediterranean is felt in the air.

For the ****PORTE DE LYON site at Dardily you come off the autoroute about 10 km. north of Lyon. It is intended as a transit site, but it is so pleasant and convenient that you may be tempted to stop there for a few days to relax and explore.

Lyon is a gracious city of splendid shops and buildings, with one of the largest town squares in France (Plâce Bellecour), and an old town of fascinating narrow streets between the river Saône and the Fourvière hill. At the top of this is the nineteenth-century Fourvière Basilica, from which there are views over the city and beyond to the Jura and Dauphiné Alps.

An interesting excursion from Lyon is along the banks of the Saône to La Rochetaillée where there is a car museum.

If you would like a change from autoroute driving you could continue south from Lyon on the other side of the Rhône, for the N.86 is an adequate road with far less traffic than the N.7 and with much less, needless to say, than the autoroute.

At Condrieu there is the ***Bel' Epoque site and also the small vineyards of the Côte Rôtie whose wines, Château-Grillet, Condrieu and Côte Rôtie you may know, although they are not as famous as those of their downstream neighbour, Châteauneuf du Pape.

Between these two groups of vineyards are the Hermitage, Crozes-Hermitage, St. Joseph and Cornas wine villages.

Between Condrieu and Tournon on the N.86 is a pleasant small site in the Castels et Camping Caravaning chain; not a top star site in the chain, but adequate and agreeably situated above the Rhône. This is the ***Château de Peyraud near Serrières about 50 km. south of Lyons. You are away from the bustle of holiday traffic here.

If you wished to explore Ardèche you could make a slight deviation from Tournon

There are valleys and rocky caverns in Ardèche

on the N.534 to the **LA CHEZE site at Le Cheylard. Ardèche is noted for extinct volcanoes and rocky caverns. Caravanning potholers will find here the deepest caverns in Europe. There are also many archaeological sites of interest.

SAVOIE - DAUPHINÉ

Approximate number of camping sites   200

Post no.	Département	Capital
74	Haute-Savoie	Annecy
73	Savoie	Chambéry
38	Isère	Grenoble

Routes connecting   12, 31, 36, 50

The presence of Mont-Blanc, the highest peak in Europe (15,772 ft.), in this province is a reminder that Savoie-Dauphiné is French Alps country. To the north the boundary is Lac Léman, the lake of Geneva, to the east Switzerland and Italy, in the south the mountains continue through Isère and Hautes-Alpes to the Mediterranean. To the west the mountains shelve away into the valley of the Rhône.

Savoie-Dauphiné is the province of skiing and mountain climbing, almost exclusively so, one might imagine, but this is not the case at all. The province belongs to the skier during the winter (although at the high-altitude resorts the season is extended), but in the summer the spas and lake resorts are crowded, there are flower festivals at Evian and Chamonix in June and July, thousands visit Mont Blanc and ride on the cogwheel railway up to the Mer de Glâce or in the cable cars from Chamonix across Mont Blanc to Courmayeur.

About one-fifth of the Savoie-Dauphiné camping sites stay open throughout the year and caravanning to a ski holiday is becoming increasingly popular. Buildings on permanent camping sites are all heated, but obviously you will need a properly insulated caravan, preferably one wired to take the site electricity supply for heating, lighting, etc.

My opinion of winter ski/caravan holidays is that *being* there is fun but *getting* there is not. The idea dies hard that you have only to drive south through France at any time to find the sun. There are beautifully sheltered spots, admittedly, but it can be colder in Lyon than in London at Christmas.

If you are interested in skiing you will know that the ski-centres are graded so that your choice of centre would be influenced by skiing rather than caravanning considerations.

To tow a caravan to the French Alps in winter may sound crazy and, I must confess, when you are engaged upon it you experience many moments when you conclude that you *must* be crazy. But many people do it and there is no reason why you should not if you are careful and take the necessary precautions.

SAVOIE – DAUPHINÉ

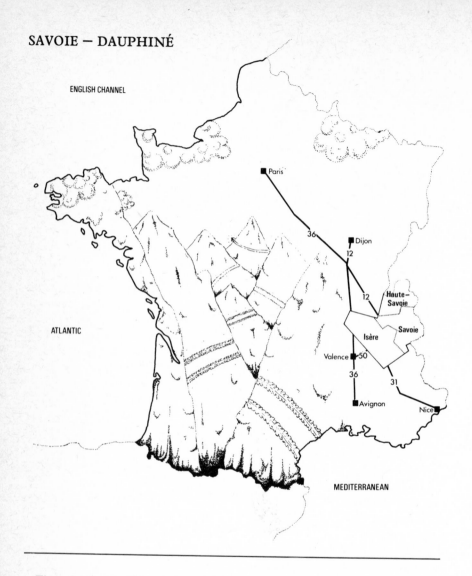

ENGLISH CHANNEL

Paris

36

Dijon

12

12

Haute–
Savoie

ATLANTIC

Isère

Savoie

Valence ■50

36

31

Avignon

Nice

MEDITERRANEAN

First of all it should be obvious that your car/caravan weight ratio must greatly favour your car. A rear-wheel-drive car will obviously have an advantage over a front-wheel-drive car, in fact the caravan nose-weight added to a rear-drive car so greatly assists traction that you have an advantage in snow over most other traffic if other considerations such as torque, weight ratio etc., are favourable. It is not an advantage that enables you to pass slower traffic, however, for deep ruts are formed in the snowy roads and you move along as though on railway lines. To attempt to pass another vehicle can be an anxious manoeuvre on such occasions. Once, above Grenoble, we tried to pass a crawling lorry and succeeded in moving

Mont Blanc

the car in the required direction, but the caravan decided to stay in the ruts and the ensuing waltz was not appreciated by oncoming traffic, even less by me.

It should hardly be necessary to mention that you should carry a spade or shovel and chains for your car. When you start climbing from dry roads up into snow you will find that the roads first become wet, then sleet-covered and then, unbelievably, you are driving in snow. If you come upon these conditions unexpectedly take the first opportunity to get off the road to fit chains; do not be tempted to carry on to find a better stopping-place for on many of the mountain roads any stopping-places at all are few and far between.

The following is a selection of camping sites that are open throughout the year:

Isère

Bourg-d'Oisans   ***LE VERNIS

Entre-Deux-Guiers   ***L'ARC-EN-CIEL

Grenoble   ***MUNICIPAL

Renage   **LE VERDON

St.-Martin-d'Uriage   **DU LUISET

St. Pierre-de-Chartreuse   **MARTINIÈRE

St. Pierrer-de-Chartreuse   *CHARMANT SOM

Seyssins   **LES 3 PUCELLES

La Terrasse   **MUNICIPAL

Savoie

Bourg-St.-Maurice   ***DU T.C.F.

Lepin-le-Lac   **LES PEUPLIERS

Trevignin   **MARLICE

Haute-Savoie

Chamonix   **LES DRUS

Chamonix   **LES ROSIERS

Chamonix is the Queen of ski resorts with 3 ski areas and a two-stage cable railway, one of the highest and longest in Europe.

Praz-sur-Arly   **CHANTALOUETTE

St. Gervais-les-Bains   ***DU DOME DE MIAGE

Thones   **LE LACHAT

In the summer the lakes and the spas, the mountains with their breathtaking views and pure air, the flowers and festivals make Savoie-Dauphiné an exciting place for an unusual caravan holiday.

At Evian-les-Bains you can site your caravan by Lake Geneva, Europe's largest lake. Another beautiful lakeside situation is at Annecy where there is the choice of half a dozen sites with the twelfth-century castle dominating the town nearby. The principal lakeside resort is Aix-les-Bains with three camping sites on Lac du Bourget and the most fashionable spa resort in France to explore.

For the thrill of 'mountain caravanning' one of the nearest sites to Mont-Blanc is the **Municipal or the **Megève-Camping at Megève where all the Beautiful People go for the fantastic night-life, the ***Le Mont Blanc Carno at Passy or one of the half dozen sites at Les Bossons.

Caravanning in the Savoie-Dauphiné is an experience that you will never forget. It will cause your car to puff a little here and there but you, at least, will be completely rejuvenated.

LANGUEDOC - ROUSSILLON

Approximate number of camping sites 300

Post no.	Département	Capital
48	Lozère	Mende
30	Gard	Nîmes
34	Hérault	Montpellier
11	Aude	Carcassonne
66	Pyrénées-Orientales	Perpignan

Routes connecting 8, 24, 25, 30, 32, 49

The greatest concentration of camping sites is around the coastal area from the Spanish border to the Camargue. This coastal area has been selected by the French Government for the Languedoc-Roussillon Development, to make it 'the greatest leisure area in the world'. There are many *étangs*, or salt-water lagoons by the sea, and the accent at the moment is on the creation of marinas with surrounding apartment blocks, shops and holiday amenities. New provision for the touring caravanner does not feature very prominently at the moment; perhaps there needs to be some life breathed into the development area first.

The centres so far developed, like La Grande Motte and Leucate-Barcarès, are oases in a desert of poor quality sand and scrub. When the wind blows (and it has a nasty and recurring habit of blowing in the Gulf of Lions), this developing coastal strip can be desolate indeed.

The established towns are attractive enough; Collioure, for instance, is everyone's idea of a dream Mediterranean resort. Next to it, along towards the Spanish border, is the colourful fishing and commercial harbour of Port Vendres with the convenient **La Presqu' ile site; equally convenient is the ***Stade camping site at next door Banyuls-sur-Mer, set in a bay of blue sea against a background of purple mountains. On the other side of Collioure there are fifty camping sites at Argèles-sur-Mer; fifty sites in one resort may attract you or deter you but the presence of so many proves that this coast must have something to recommend it.

If you are tucked in comfortably on a site on this coast you would find Perpignan a good tourist centre, excellent alike for shopping or history according to taste. From here you can explore up into the Pyrénées. It is only about 100 km. to the smallest state in Europe, the republic of Andorra, squatting up in the mountains between France and Spain. There are a dozen or so camping sites in Andorra; there are also altitudes of up to 8,000 ft. and the highest pass in Europe. The principal sites are along the main road from France into Spain and there are quite a number in the capital, Andorra la Vella. Mostly they are crowded transit camps, dusty and not completely restful by any means.

LANGUEDOC – ROUSSILLON

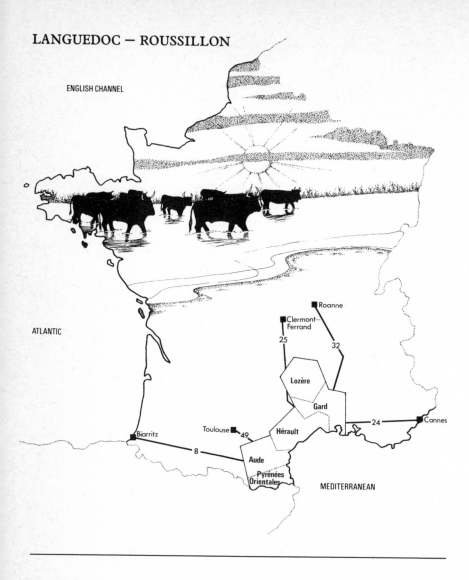

ENGLISH CHANNEL

ATLANTIC

Roanne

Clermont–
Ferrand

25

32

Lozère

Gard

Toulouse

49

Hérault

24

Cannes

Biarritz

8

Aude

Pyrénées
Orientales

MEDITERRANEAN

Between Andorra and Perpignan there are mountain strongholds, remote abbeys, seemingly neglected villages, olive trees, mimosa and, of course, the vineyards that produce the wines of Roussillon. The Catalan town of Prades, by Mt. Canigou, is entertaining; here and at the nearby spa of Amélie-les-Bains-Palalda you might see Catalan dancing. The **LE GAOU and **MUNICIPAL sites at Amélie are convenient but there are other camping sites throughout Roussillon.

The medieval city of Carcassonne, with its battlements and fifty towers, seems to rise out of the Languedoc plain, particularly when floodlit. The camping site here

Sète . . . the beach

is the ***CAMPING A. DOMEC on the River Aude or ***Camping les Lavandières, 4 km. away at Pennautier on the River Frésquel.

There are many charming, historic towns in Languedoc-Roussillon, Narbonne for instance, ancient capital of South Gaul, and Béziers. The **Le Rebau site at Montblanc is pleasant and conveniently near.

Some of the camping sites are more dramatically situated in the Gorges du Tarn area between Millau and Mende; apart from this, the upper part of the département of Lozère is not noted for its holiday liveliness.

Montpellier and Hérault generally offer many attractions to the tourist including Roman remains, Gothic architecture, mountains and rivers, also interesting harbour resorts at Agde and Sète. There are many camping sites all along the coast.

You may see a bullfight at Nîmes. It is a beautiful town with a remarkably well-preserved Roman arena and amphitheatre. Away behind are the Cévennes mountains, towards the Mediterranean is the Camargue with swamps and lagoons, white horses and fighting bulls and flamingoes. There are no camping sites actually in the Camargue, the nearest being the ***La Marine at Le Grau-du-Poi/Port Camargue plus a number of others here or the *****Louis Pibols or *****Le Garden at La Grande Motte already mentioned.

Languedoc-Roussillon has something of everything for a successful caravan holiday.

PROVENCE – CÔTE D'AZUR

Approximate number of camping sites   300

Post no.	Département	Capital
84	Vaucluse	Avignon
05	Hautes-Alpes	Gap
04	Alpes de Haute Provence	Digne
13	Bouches-du-Rhône	Marseille
83	Var	Draguignan

Routes connecting   6, 16, 24, 30, 31, 36

The pause at Lyon suggested in the Vallée du Rhône section for caravanners who are making the long haul to the Mediterranean could equally well be taken at Avignon. In the limited time of an annual holiday it is understandable that the magic of the Mediterranean should claim priority; but it is still a pity to rush past the glories of Avignon, Arles and Orange.

The autoroute by-passes Avignon, but only a small deviation is required to visit the ****MUNICIPAL site there. You would find it restful and refreshing to visit the Palace of the Popes, to look down from the palace gardens at the Rhône barges swirling round the bend to pass the remains of the famous bridge at Avignon; better still to see the palace at night, floodlit and filled with sound.

Across the river you would be welcomed at the 'home' of one of the most famous wines in the world, Châteauneuf du Pape, already mentioned.

If you spared another day or so there are Roman monuments, theatres, arches, baths, arenas at Orange and Arles as well as many others, also châteaux, palaces and museums, bullfights and festivals.

Below Avignon the usual route to the Mediterranean branches off towards Aix-en-Provence and many caravanners do not approach close to the sea until nearing St. Raphael. Admittedly the immediate coastal vicinity of Marseille is not very inspiring, but Bandol and Sanary are beautiful little resorts with excellent camping sites and Hyères and the Giens peninsula are full of holiday interest. The ****Domaine du Ceinturon site at Ayguade-Ceinturon, just outside Hyères, is a most attractive centre from which to explore. There is not such a sardine-packed holiday intensity at Hyères as there is at other resorts.

The coast from Le Lavandou to Agay is generously supplied with camping sites by the sea. To rise from your bed, put on your swimming trunks, open the caravan door and plunge straight into the blue Mediterranean is heaven indeed; the trouble is that between mid-July and the end of August the rest of the world seems to have the same idea.

Before trying a beside-the-sea camping site for the first time be warned that the

PROVENCE — CÔTE D'AZUR

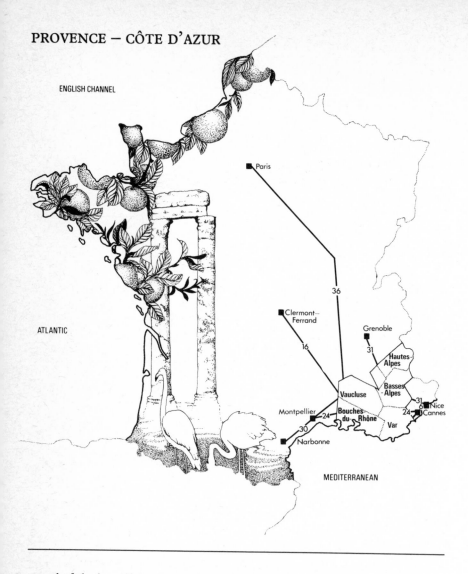

ENGLISH CHANNEL

Paris

Clermont—
Ferrand

Grenoble

Hautes-
Alpes

Basses
-Alpes

ATLANTIC

Vaucluse

Montpellier

Bouches
du–Rhône

Nice

Cannes

Var

Narbonne

MEDITERRANEAN

sound of the beautiful sea can rob you of sleep; also, there is rarely any shade at the seaside sites and the heat of the sun during the day can turn your caravan into an oven. The height of the season is usually the height of the heat and then a resigned lethargy descends upon you as you move from queue to queue, for toilets, showers, water, camp-shop, everything.

You may prefer to seek a shaded grassy site a little way back from the Mediterranean if you are caravanning in Provence-Côte d'Azur at the height of the season, perhaps towards the foothills of the mountains of the Maures and the Estérel. Or you may decide upon one of the sites near to the River Durance, in which case you would be within reasonable distance of the Mediterranean and also of Aix-en-Provence at the centre of classical Provence. To the west you would be able to explore the Camargue, where the Rhône divides, a strange and remote area of bird sanctuaries.

For the free-and-easy caravanner there can be much more to Provence-Côte d'Azur than the sea.

Cowboys in the forum . . . Arles

RIVIERA – CÔTE D'AZUR

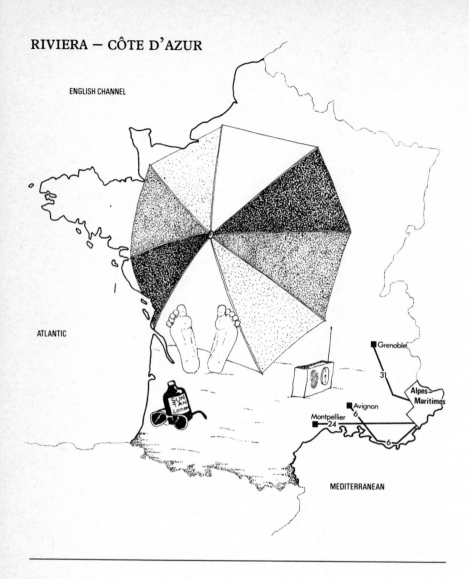

ENGLISH CHANNEL

ATLANTIC

Grenoble

31

Alpes
Maritimes

Avignon
6

Montpellier
24

6

MEDITERRANEAN

RIVIERA – CÔTE D'AZUR

Approximate number of camping sites   120

Post no.	Département	Capital
06	Alpes-Maritime	Nice

Routes connecting   6, 24, 31

Nice; carnival

There are many ***** camping sites beside the sea, but in July and August they are crowded, all holiday facilities are packed, and all the coast roads are absolutely jammed. At the same time the Côte d'Azur is fabulous or frightful depending upon your point of view. And sites that are *really* near to the sea inevitably have the railway line and coast road *really* near to them.

If you are obliged to take your holidays between mid-July and the end of August you might prefer to seek a camping site a little way back from the sea, say at the *****DOMAINE DE LA BERGERIE at Vence, the ***Les Gorges du Loup at Le Bar-sur-Loup, the ****LOU PISTOU at St. Laurent-du-Var, the *****Du Verdon, ****Lac de Castillon or ***St.-Michel at Castellane. Nowhere in this province is far away: you can drive either to the blue Mediterranean or to the snowy peaks in under two hours. The **CHAMPOUNS site at St. Martin-Vésubie is open all the year.

You drive amidst palm trees, orange and aloe, cactus and eucalyptus, rose-laurel, bougainvillea and mimosa; the vegetation is tropical and the winter temperatures high because of the protective screen of mountains.

In about 100 km. of coastline there are twenty-six resorts, many with marinas and some with more than one, the yacht harbour at Cannes being the largest in the world.

If you can manage it the best time to visit the Côte d'Azur is at some time other than July/August, which is not synonymous with 'out of season' on this coast for it is not so long ago that the best hotels actually closed during the summer months. Nice Carnival starts twelve days before Shrove Tuesday, the Mimosa Festival at Cannes is in February, as is the Lemon Festival at Menton.

Enough beautiful camping sites are open all the year round here to enable you to take your caravan holiday when you like. If you are retired and have the blessed gift of time why winter in England when you could be eating your Christmas pudding in the sunshine of the Côte d'Azur?

CORSICA

Corsica is a most beautiful island but many of the scenic roads are quite unsuitable for towing a caravan. The beautiful coastal road from Ajaccio to Calvi, for instance, is positively alarming, with hairpin bend after hairpin bend, so much so that it is never possible to get above third gear and not often above second; with dips down into valleys and climbs up to mountain sides, unprotected road edges with loose stone surfaces bordering them. There is little traffic certainly, but what there is seems to be composed of crazy truck drivers dicing with their death and yours.

If you wish to visit Corsica it is best to leave your caravan on the mainland, say at the beautiful *****LA BERGERIE site at Vence, above Nice Airport. You can leave your car in the long-stay park at the airport and fly Air France to Corsica in forty minutes. If you prefer to travel by sea the steamers leave Nice (and other ports) regularly and the journey takes seven hours.

It is possible to hire cars at many points in Corsica. At the airports and ports all the international car hire firms are represented and many others. You can, of course hire a car, say, at Ajaccio and leave it at Bastia if you wish, arranging your arrival and departure from these different points.

Part III

ROUTES THROUGH FRANCE

10 GAZETTEER OF PLACE-NAMES

The numbers are those of the Author's suggested routes.

131

II ITINERARIES

*Caravan/Camping sites printed in lowercase (small) letters, e.g. *Municipal **St. Jean ***Le Haut-Dyk ****La Chêneraie, are open for certain months of each year. Annual guides give a good indication of the current opening dates although they are not 100 per cent reliable.*

*Caravan/Camping sites printed in capitals, e.g. *MUNICIPAL **DU PONT ***LES PRUNIERS ****CHANTECLER, are open permanently.*

Route I ABBEVILLE – DIEPPE – ROUEN – ALENÇON – (AVRANCHES) – RENNES

MICHELIN MAP NO.	ROAD NO. CARAVAN SITES	Km.	
52	**N.28** **RENDEZ-VOUS DES CAMPEURS *RELAIS DU PONTHIEU		*Somme* **ABBEVILLE (Connect Route 17)** On the Somme; was the H.Q. of British troops in WWI and was almost destroyed in WW2. St. Vulfran, 15thC; Château de Bagatelle, 18thC, Louis XV furniture.
	**MUNICIPAL	25	*Seine Maritime* **BLANGY-SUR-BRESLE**
		30	**NEUFCHÂTEL-EN-BRAY** Rebuilt after being destroyed in WW2.
	N.15 **CAMP DU PRE SAINT-NICOLAS **Le Pollet	36	**DIEPPE** An interesting old town, with a long boulevard above the shingle beach and a fishing and commercial harbour, situated at the mouth of the River Arques. St. Jacques, 12thC; Dieppe Castle, 15thC; Museum: Sculpture, ship models, souvenirs of the composer Saint-Saëns.

	N.28		
	***LA MALMAISON	28	**PIERREVAL**

55 **ROUEN-BONSECOURS** 17 **ROUEN (Connect Routes 19, 42, 43, 44)**

Capital of Seine Maritime. Although 128 km. up the Seine, Rouen is the third seaport in France with 24 km. of docks and wharves. It is an important industrial town specializing in textiles. It was much damaged in WW2. Joan of Arc was burned alive in Rouen in 1431; the site on the Place du Vieux-Marche is marked and there is a statue nearby of Joan at the stake. Notre-Dame Cath., 13thC. Museums – Beaux Arts: Corot, Delacroix, Fragonard, Monet, Poussin, Renoir, Sisley. Antiquities: Natural History: Ironwork.

54 **N.138**
*Municipal

Eure

30 **BRIONNE**

On the River Risle. Castle ruins, 12thC; St. Martin, 15thC.

55 15 **BERNAY**

St. Cross, 14thC; Notre-Dame, 15thC; Museum: Rouen, Nevers and Strasbourg china; Norman furniture.

Orne

70 **SEES**

60 **JACQUES FOULD** 22 **ALENÇON (Connect Route 2)**

Capital of Orne, a market town on the River Sarthe, noted for the manufacture of lace (Alençon point). Birthplace of St. Teresa, 1873; there are pilgrimages to her house, now a chapel. School of Lace, sales shop and display; Art Gallery, lace and paintings; Castle, 14thC; St. Leonard's, 14thC; Museum in Ozé House, 15thC; fortified gateway, 15thC.

N.12

Mayenne

25 **PRÉ-EN-PAIL**

59 **N.807**
**Municipal Les Mares

Manche

100 **AVRANCHES**

A pleasant town full of flowers and with many historical associations, though most of its visitors are attracted by nearby Mont-St.-Michel. In the square at Avranches is a stone, known as The Platform, where Henry II knelt to receive absolution (having been excommunicated following the murder of Thomas à Becket). More recently a monument was erected to General Patton who led the WW2 U.S. attack from here. Botanical Gardens, floodlit in summer; Museum; Patton monument.

Mont-St.-Michel

****Camp du Mont-St.-Michel
**Le Gué de Beauvoir
**Sous les Pommiers

MONT-ST.-MICHEL

A 'marvel' or 'wonder' as the brochure rightly claims, is a sight to take your breath away; a small island with a lower surround of medieval walls, with houses climbing up the sides and completely surmounted by a thousand-year-old monastery. Seen from afar, standing out from the shining wastes of sand, it is said to resemble the Great Pyramid; looking down from the island at the tide advancing over the sand at speed is an unforgettable experience. Tide tables are issued free by the Syndicat d'Initiative. The best time to come is just after a full moon or new moon; the rise and fall of tide is the greatest in Europe. There are restaurants, hotels and souvenir shops in the one street.

N.12
***Municipal

12 **JAVRON**

**RAYMOND-FAUQUE

25 **MAYENNE**

A textile manufacturing town on hills above the River Mayenne. Much damaged in WW2 and rebuilt on attractive lines. Notre-Dame, part-12thC; Castle dating back to William the Conqueror.

*CAMPING DE L'AVANT-GARDE LAIQUE

Ile et Vilaine

45 **FOUGERES**

An industrial town, noted for the manufacture of shoes, situated above the Nançon valley and over-looking the impressive castle that dates back to the 11thC. Much damaged in WW2. St. Sulpice, 15thC.

**LA FORÊT

17 **LIFFRE**

30 **RENNES (Connect Routes 34, 45)**

Principal town of Ile-et-Vilaine and situated where the two rivers join. Damaged in WW2, Rennes is not exactly a colourful place except, perhaps, for the gardens by the quays alongside the River Vilaine. There is a lot of industry here but it is an agricultural centre too. Notre-Dame, 12thC. Museums – Beaux-Arts: Latour, Poussin. Archaeology: Breton Folk Art.

Route 2 ALENÇON – TOURS

MICHELIN MAP NO.	ROAD NO. CARAVAN SITES	Km.	
	N.138		*Orne*
60	★★JACQUES FOULD		**ALENÇON (Connect Route 1)**
			Sarthe
	★★Sans Souci	20	**FRESNAY-SUR-SARTHE**
	★★Val de Sarthe	25	**BEAUMONT-SUR-SARTHE**
	★CAMP ST.-EXUPÉRY	27	**LE MANS (Connect Routes 29, 34)**

On the Rivers Sarthe and Huisme. Because it is so well known for the June 24-hour motor race it is sometimes overlooked that Le Mans has a considerable history. King Henry II of England was born here in 1133. It was an important city in pre-Roman times. Notre-Dame, 13thC; St. Julian Cath., 11thC. Musée des Beaux Arts: David, Delacroix, Latour.

The cathedral at Le Mans

MICHELIN MAP NO.	ROAD NO. CARAVAN SITES	Km.	
	N.158	21	**ECOMMOY**
64	**Du Coemont	20	**CHÂTEAU-DU-LOIR**
	**MUNICIPAL	6	**DISSAY-SOUS-COURCILLON**
			Indre-et-Loire
		15	**NEUILLE-PONT-PIERRE**
	**Camp de la Choisille	14	**LA MEMBROLLE-SUR-CHOISILLE**
	**DE L'ALOUETTE	7	**TOURS (Connect Routes 4, 13, 37)**

TOURS (Connect Routes 4, 13, 37)

Chief town of Indre-et-Loire and one-time capital of Touraine. Known as the Garden of France, it is in the centre of the Châteaux country. In the church of St. Martin is an enormous statue of the saint who was Bishop of Tours in the year 370 and whose missionary zeal resulted in many churches being named after him (including St. Martin-in-the-Fields). It is a prosperous and interesting town in the centre of the region of royal castles. St. Gatien Cath., 12thC; St. Julien, 13thC. Beaux Arts Museum: Rubens, Rembrandt, Boucher, Delacroix, Degas; period furniture. Remains of the Tour de Guise, 12thC. To the west is Le Plessis-les-Tours where Louis XI died in 1488; now a museum of the silk industry of Touraine.

The Châteaux of the Loire area extends from Angers to Gien, a distance of 600 km. It would take a week of sightseeing to visit all the attractions of this region, more if the programme was timed to include the many illuminated spectacles, the son et lumière shows that re-create history so vividly.

From Angers to Tours is described in **Route 4** and from Tours to Orléans in **Route 37**.

Route 3 ANGERS – CHOLET – LES SABLES D'OLONNE

MICHELIN MAP NO.	ROAD NO. CARAVAN SITES	Km.	

63 | **N.161**
| | **★★PARC DE LA HAYE** | | *Maine-et-Loire*

ANGERS (Connect Routes 4, 29)
One-time capital of Anjou and now of Maine-et-Loire, noted for the Castle of Angers and for its tapestry. Angers was a capital in pre-Roman times. It is a prosperous and attractive place with gardens, flowers and fine houses. It is divided by the River Maine. The castle has 17 round towers and was built in the 13thC; once the home of the Counts of Anjou whose descendants founded the Plantagenet dynasty. In the Museum of Tapestry the principal exhibit, the Apocalypse, is over 500 ft. long and over 500 years old. Angers is noted for Loire wines and for Cointreau liqueur; the Cointreau Distillery is open daily to the public. Gothic St. Maurice Cath., 12thC. Musée Logis Barrault, 14thC: sculptures, 18thC French paintings. Hôpital St. Jean, 12thC, built by Henry II in penance for the murder of Thomas à Becket; houses tapestries of the Chant du Monde and a wine museum.

6 **PONTS DE CE**

30 **CHEMILLE**

67 | **N.160** | 23 **CHOLET**
Noted for its big cattle market, one of the most important in France.

Angers

MICHELIN MAP NO.	ROAD NO. CARAVAN SITES	Km.	

Vendée

		10	**MORTAGNE-S-SEVRE (Connect Route 28)**
*DE ROMAINE			
		15	**LES HERBIERS**
		20	**LES ESSARTS**
*MUNICIPAL		20	**LA ROCHE-S-YON**

*DE ROMAINE

10 **MORTAGNE-S-SEVRE (Connect Route 28)**

15 **LES HERBIERS**

20 **LES ESSARTS**

*MUNICIPAL

20 **LA ROCHE-S-YON**

Principal town of the Vendée and a holiday centre for exploring that part of the Loire Valley.

18 **LA MOTHE-ACHARD**

***La Baie de Cayola
***Les Fosses Rouges
***Camp des Roses

17 **LES SABLES D'OLONNE**

A fishing port and typical holiday town with a splendid sandy beach, a fine promenade, Casino and a daily fish auction at the harbour.

This coast is more popular with French than with English tourists who are drawn by the magnet of the Mediterranean. The Atlantic coast is invigorating, enjoys a splendid climate, is rich in historical association and is less crowded than the Mediterranean resorts.

Route 4 ANGERS — TOURS — VIERZON — BOURGES — NEVERS — MÂCON

The 'Châteaux of the Loire' area extends from Angers to Giens, a distance of 600 km. This route 4 covers the Châteaux area as far as Tours and then branches off; from Orléans to Tours is described in Route 37.

The Camp sites shown are on the road traversed but there are many more in the area.

The châteaux shown are on the route or nearby; nowhere else in the world is there such a fabulous concentration of castles and history.

MICHELIN MAP NO.	ROAD NO. CARAVAN SITES	Km.	
63	N.152 **PARC DE LA HAYE		*Maine-et-Loire* ANGERS (Connect Routes 3, 29)
	**Municipal	19	ST. MATHURIN
	**Port St. Maur	4	LA MENITRE
	**Municipal	7	LES ROSIERS
	**Municipal	7	ST. MARTIN-DE-LA-PLACE
	***MUNICIPAL	8	SAUMUR

An attractive town on the Loire, a crossing-place and a meeting-place for a thousand years. In the 14thC castle above the town is a museum devoted to the history of horses. The Cavalry School gives riding displays at the end of July. A local industry is the making of medals but Saumur is chiefly famous for its sparkling wine. Notre-Dame, 12thC, Romanesque with 15thC tapestries; Château de Saumur, 14thC; Military Museum. Nearby Fontevrault Abbey, 11thC, houses the tombs of the Plantagenets.

(Following this N.152 Route from Saumur to Tours an alternative route is given taking in other châteaux)

67	N.152 **Port-Roux	4	VILLEBERNIER
		38	*Indre-et-Loire* LANGEAIS

The Château de Langeais, 15thC, was built by Louis XI as a fortress and is situated in a prominent position in the centre of the town.

		5	CINQ-MARS-LA-PILE

The 'pile' in the place-name does not refer to the nearby atomic power station but to the Gallo-Roman pylon structure on the hill. From the small château there are splendid views over the Loire Valley.

9 **LUYNES**
A pleasant village dominated by the 13thC Château de Luynes.

64 ★★DE L'ALOUETTE 25 **TOURS (Connect Route 2)**

Alternative route from Saumur to Tours *Maine-et-Loire*
SAUMUR

N.147
★★★Isle Verte 11 **MONTSOREAU**
A pretty village with a 15thC château. Museum: historical.

N.751 2 **CANDES-ST.-MARTIN**
An old village, once fortified, at the junction of the Loire and the Vienne. 12thC church.

15 **ST. LAZAIRE**

Indre-et-Loire
★★★Municipal 2 **CHINON**
In a beautiful situation on the River Loire, famous for

Saumur, on the Loire

the Château du Milieu, 11thC, and the Château du Coudray where Joan of Arc stayed when she saw Charles VII in 1429. There are picturesque houses in the older part of the town; nearby, in contrast, is a nuclear power station.
(8 miles north, on D.16, is the Château d'Ussé, a white castle at the edge of a dark forest, the Castle of the Sleeping Beauty, built in the 16thC.)

N.751
***Parc du Sabot   21   **AZAY-LE-RIDEAU**
A charming little town with a 16thC château containing a Renaissance museum.
(A slight detour on D.39 is worth while to see the unique terraced gardens of the Renaissance château of Villandry)

27   **TOURS (Connect Routes 2, 13, 37)**

N.76
*La Duvallerie   15   **AZAY-SUR-CHER**

***Municipal   12   **BLERE**

64   8   **CHENONCEAUX**
The Château de Chenonceaux is one of the most impressive; it is remarkable for being built across the River Cher, and it is known as the 'Château of Six Women'. Diane de Poitiers, mistress of Henry II, lived there from 1547. She was turned out on his death (1559), by his widow, Catherine de Medici.

Indre-et-Loire
5   **CHISSY-EN-TOURAINE**
The village is dominated by the 15thC château.

Loire-et-Cher
L'Etourneau   4   **MONTRICHARD
An old town above which stands a ruined keep.

17   **ST. AIGNAN-SUR-CHER**
A pretty little town with a 13thC château.
St. Aignan, 12thC.

*Municipal   2   **NOYERS-SUR-CHER**

Le Parici   1   **CHÂTILLON-SUR-CHER

MICHELIN MAP NO.	ROAD NO. CARAVAN SITES	Km.	
		12	**SELLES-SUR-CHER**
	*Municipal	18	**VILLEFRANCHE-SUR-CHER**
	**Val Rose	8	**MENNETON-SUR-CHER**
	**Les Saules	4	**CHATRES-SUR-CHER**
	**Bellon-Plage	14	*Cher* **VIERZON (Connect Route 48)** A manufacturing town and big railway centre.
	**Municipal	16	**MEHUN-SUR-YEVRE**
69	**Municipal	18	**BOURGES** Capital of Cher, at the junction of the rivers Yèvre and Auron, a market town with industries and two thousand years of history; there are many old mansions and beautiful gardens. St. Etienne, 12thC, splendid Gothic Cath. Palais Jacques Coeur, 14thC.

'The Château of Six Women' . . . Chenonceaux

		20	**AVORD**
		14	**NERONDES**
		12	**LA GUERCHE-S-L'AUBOIS**
69			*Nièvre*
	**MUNICIPAL	20	**NEVERS (Connect Route 38)**

Capital of Nièvre, noted for the manufacture of fine china, an industry that has been carried on here for over three hundred years. Situated at the junction of the Loire and Nièvre, Nevers is an interesting place with medieval streets dominated by the Cathedral of St. Cyr, 10thC, and the Ducal Palace, 15thC Renaissance.
Saint Bernadette of Lourdes died, a nun, in 1879 at St. Gildard Convent and her body is preserved there.
Museum: Nevers pottery, Limoges enamels.

N.79
****Les Halles — 34 — **DECIZE**

An old town in an island setting on the Loire. St. Aré church is built on a 7thC Merovingian crypt.
Minim monastery.

Saône-et-Loire
***La Chevrette — 66 — **DIGOIN**

An industrial town situated on the Loire and also on the Canal du Centre which here crosses an impressive aqueduct.

***Le Pré Barret — 2 — **PARAY-LE-MONIAL**

An industrial town specializing in tile manufacture and ceramics. Pilgrimages are made annually to the Basilica of the Sacred Heart, 11thC. Musée du Hieron: Romanesque tympanum.

13 — **CHAROLLES**

Above the town is the ancient former Château of the Counts of Charollais. This is a market town in farming country or cattle-rearing country; the Charollais breed of cattle has achieved world renown. There are weekly cattle sales in the summer.

****MUNICIPAL — 55 — **MÂCON (Connect Route 36)**

A centre of the wine-growing industry on the Saône (1,000 ft. wide here); a port from which shipping can reach the Mediterranean. Birthplace of Lamartine.

Route 5 ANGOULÊME – MONTLUÇON – MOULINS – DIJON – NANCY

MICHELIN MAP NO.	ROAD NO. CARAVAN SITES	Km.	

72	N.141 ***BOURGINES		*Charente* **ANGOULÊME (Connect Route 13)** Capital of Charente, once part of the Roman Empire and agreeably situated on the River Charente. A manufacturing town, particularly of paper, much damaged in WW2. Birthplace of Marguerite de Valois, Queen of Navarre. Rich in historical buildings. Cath. St. Pierre, 11thC; Gothic Town Hall built on the site of the Castle of the Counts of Angoulême – the Polygon, 13thC, and de Valois, 15thC, towers remain.
	*Les Flots	22	**LA ROCHEFOUCAULD** There is an 11thC castle here, a one-time owner of which, the Duc de Rochefoucauld, wrote the Book of Maxims. St. Florent, 11thC.
		12	**CHASSENEUIL-S-BONNIEURE**
	N.151 BIS **Les Ribières	30	**CONFOLENS**
		18	*Haute Vienne* **MEZIERS-S-ISSOIRE**
	***Les Rochettes	12	**BELLAC** A small town on the River Vincou.
	N.142	31	*Creuse* **LA CROISERE**
		9	**LA SOUTERRAINE** There is a Gallic fort here and 11thC houses.
		22	**ST. VAURY**
	**Municipal	12	**GUÉRET** A pretty little place with an interesting museum containing Aubusson tapestries, also pictures, and Gallo-Roman antiquities. St. Pierre, 13thC.
	N.145	31	**GOUZON**

69			*Allier*
	**LE MAS	34	**MONTLUÇON (Connect Route 41)**
	*Municipal		An important industrial centre; the industry is on one side of the River Cher and on the other side is the old town with steep, narrow streets of half-timbered houses crowned by a castle, formerly the property of the Bourbon dukes. St. Pierre, 12thC; Notre-Dame, 15thC. Château de Montluçon, museum: ceramics.
	**Le Boutillon	9	**CHAMBLET (Connect Route 41)**
		22	**MONTMARAULT (Connect Route 41)**
		31	**SOUVIGNY**
			An ancient town in a picturesque mountain setting on the left slope of the Queune valley, with the finest and most intriguing church in the Bourbonnais, St. Pierre, 11thC, containing the tombs of the Bourbon dukes.
	**Camping-Plage	12	**MOULINS (Connect Route 38)**
			On the River Allier, capital of Allier and, five hundred years ago, capital of the Bourbonnais. An imposing town with half-timbered houses and a museum that was part of the Ducal Palace (local pottery, paintings and a Souvigny Bible). Clock Tower, 14thC; Gothic Notre-Dame Cath., 14thC.
	N.73 ***St. Prix	36	*Saône-et-Loire* **BOURBON-LANCY**
			Situated nearly 1,000 ft. up and looking over the Loire and Burgundy. There is a spa here for the treatment of rheumatism. St. Nazaire, 11thC; Clock Tower, 15thC; Museum: antiquities.
		27	*Nièvre* **LUZY**
	**Municipal	34	*Saône-et-Loire* **AUTUN**
			In the Middle Ages Autun was known for its cathedral, built in the 12thC to house the relics of St. Lazarus, the friend of Jesus. Autun is a fascinating old city in a pretty situation on the River Arroux. There is some industry. St. Lazare Cath., 12thC; St. Lazare fountain, 1543. Roman Gates, remains of the largest theatre in Roman Gaul; Temple of Janus, 1stC AD; Natural History Museum, one of the richest in France.

N.494		*Côte d'Or*
**DE FOUCHE	17	**ARNAY-LE-DUC**
N.77 Bis	28	**SOMBERNON**

66

N.5
***CAMPING DU LAC   20 **DIJON (Connect Routes 12, 18)**
***L'Orée du Bois

A busy commercial town whose history goes back to
Roman times. In the 15thC the Dukes of Burgundy
made it a chief centre of European civilization. Dijon
is at the start of the Côte d'Or, the world-famous
wine-growing area noted for Côtes de Beaune, Côtes
des Nuits and Côtes de Chalon.
Notre-Dame, 12thC; St. Bénigne Cath., 13thC.
Musée des Beaux Arts: Latour, Manet, Rubens, Hals,
Veronese. Musée Magnin: Chardin, David, Fragonard,
Manet, Poussin, Rubens, La Tour. Archaeological
Museum; Musée Rude: major works of the Dijon
sculptor, François Rude.

N.74
Haute-Marne
56 **LONGEAU (Connect Route 21)**

Navarre   11 **LANGRES (Connect Routes 7, 21)
**La Liez

On a hill overlooking the Marne valley, one of the few
fortified towns to retain its original character. The
ancient walls around the town have six doors in the
ramparts, one, the Porte des Moulins, dating from
1647. Diderot was born here.
St. Mammès Cath., 12thC; St. Martin, 13thC. Musée
de l'Hotel du Breuil: early pottery, furniture, cutlery
(for which Langres is famous), souvenirs of Diderot.
Musée St. Didier: Gallo-Roman antiquities, paintings,
Gillot, Ziegler, Tassel.

*Du Château   23 **MONTIGNY-LE-ROI**

62

*Municipal   *Vosges*
49 **NEUFCHÂTEAU**

Picturesque old place situated above the Meuse.
St. Nicholas, 12thC; St. Christophe, 13thC.

Meurthe-et-Moselle
26 **COLOMBEY-LES-BELLES**

20 **PONT ST. VINCENT**

MICHELIN MAP NO.	ROAD NO. CARAVAN SITES	Km.	
	***DE BRABOIS	15	**NANCY (Connect Routes 26, 33, 39)** On the River Meurthe and the Rhine–Marne Canal, capital of the département and one-time capital of Lorraine, a city of 18thC art. Although principally commercial it is a very elegant town with fine buildings and squares, the Place d'Alliance, the ancient quarters around the Ducal Palace and the Place Stanislaus surrounded by five palaces. Musée des Beaux Arts: Boucher, Delacroix, Manet, Tintoretto, Rubens, Jordaens.

Nancy

Route 6 AVIGNON – MARSEILLE – TOULON – ST. TROPEZ – CANNES – NICE – MONTE CARLO – MENTON

MICHELIN MAP NO.	ROAD NO. CARAVAN SITES	Km.	
81	**N.7**		*Vaucluse*
80	★★★★MUNICIPAL		**AVIGNON (Connect Routes 16, 30, 36)**
	★★★BAGATELLE		One of the great cities of France, dominated by the Palace of the Popes and enclosed within massive walls. Notre-Dame Cath., 12thC; St. Ruf, 12thC; St. Agricol, 14thC; St. Pierre, 14thC. The famous St. Bénezet bridge of the song, 'Sur le pont d'Avignon L'on y danse tout en rond' was built in the 12thC and half of it was demolished five hundred years later. Musée Calvet: Corot, David, Daumier, Dufy, Manet, Le Nain, Poussin, Sisley, Toulouse-Lautrec, Utrillo.
84	★★★St. Andiol	18	**ST. ANDIOL**
81	★★★L'HIPPODROME	2	**CAVAILLON**
84			*Bouches du Rhône*
	★LES CERISIERS	3	**PLAN D'ORGON**
	★★NOSTRADAMUS	21	**SALON-DE-PROVENCE (Connect Route 24)** A cheerful little market town with an old quarter of narrow streets. Nostradamus, 15thC astrologer, lived here and is buried in St. Laurent church, 14thC. Château de l'Empéri, 13thC, is now a splendid Military Museum.
	A.7 ★★EUROPE ★★LE CASTOR	30	**VITROLLES**
	★★★LES IRIS ★★MAZARGUES ★Bonneveine	31	**MARSEILLE** Oldest and second largest city in France and capital of Bouches-du-Rhône, its origins go back to the 6thC BC. An important commercial and industrial city, the centre of its life and activity is the large harbour, the Vieux Port dominated by the Basilica of Notre-Dame de la Garde. Up from the Vieux Port leads one of the most famous thoroughfares in the world, the Cannebière, a long, wide street of shops and restaurants. Museums: Coins, Marseilles and Provence china, sculptures, paintings, Natural History, marine, Egypt and the Orient. Zoological Garden with a variety of birds.

MICHELIN MAP NO.	ROAD NO. CARAVAN SITES	Km.	
84	***CLAIRE FONTAINE	12	**AUBAGNE**
	N.559		
	**CLOS DES CIGALES	12	**CASSIS** A picturesque fishing port with the highest cliff in France (Cap Canaille, 1,365 ft.). The area is famous for the 'calanques' resembling fjords.
	***Val d'Azur ***LA TREILLE ***Les Oliviers **La Bastide Rose **ST. JEAN **LE CLOS DU RÊVE	12	**LA CIOTAT** Described as a health resort, but somewhat dominated by a huge shipyard; beyond, a long seafront promenade backs on to pine-covered hills. In the old town 17th and 18thC houses lean together in a fascinating jumble. Ciotaden Museum: local and maritime history.

Marseille

	Km.	
		Var
***LES BAUMELLES	10	**ST. CYR SUR MER**
***VAL D'ARAN	8	**BANDOL**
**VALLONGUE		A charming little holiday resort and fishing port.
**MUNICIPAL		Casino, Botanical Gardens, Zoo, Wine Museum.
****Les Girelles	6	**SANARY-SUR-MER**
**Mogador		A year-round seaside and health resort with splendid beaches sheltered by wooded cliffs. Saracen tower, 11thC.
****Le Rayolet	3	**SIX-FOURS**
***MER ET MONTAGNE		
***ST. JEAN		
***HELIOSPORTS		
***Les Charmettes		
****Les Pins	5	**LA SEYNE-SUR-MER**
***MIMOSAS		
**L'UNION		
**LES FONTANETTES		

6 **TOULON**
The principal naval town of France with a great deal of interest around the harbour, and what has been called the finest roadstead in the world. The old part of the town is fascinating, with narrow streets and little squares. It is the H.Q. of the Mediterranean Fleet; during WW2 many ships were scuttled in the harbour to avoid capture and there was much damage generally. St. Marie-Majeure Cath., 11thC. Museum: 17th and 18thC paintings and naval section.

84

****Domaine du Ceinturon (at Ayguade)	24	**HYÈRES**
***St. Pierre-des-Horts		

Famous since the 18thC as a winter and summer resort and enjoying one of the most moderate climates in France, Hyères is a town of palm trees and steep, narrow streets. R. L. Stevenson spent the happiest years of his life here (a plaque marks the house), and here he wrote *A Child's Garden of Verses*, *Prince Otto* and *Black Arrow*. Olbius-Riquier Gardens, 16 acres of many rare plants.

***Miramar	9	**LA LONDE LES MAURES**
***La Pascalinette		

***Le Pansard

****Parc de Bormes   10   **BORMES-LES-MIMOSAS**
**Manjastre

A winter and summer resort in a typically Provençal setting.

****Les Mimosas   3   **LE LAVANDOU**
***Helio Martin
**St. Pons
*Rayon d'Or

Popular resort summer and winter. There are splendid beaches and boat trips to the islands of Porquerolles and Port Cros. The Ile du Levant is a nudist colony.

***Parc Camping de   7   **CAVALIÈRE**
   Pramousquier

****La Baie   14   **CAVALAIRE-SUR-MER**
****LA PINÈDE
***Du Cros du Mouton

A delightful holiday resort with a fine sandy beach over two miles long sheltered by pine-covered hills.

***Camping Roux

****Selection Camping   6   **LA CROIX VALMER**

N.98
****PARC MONTANA   2   **GASSIN**

A Moorish village with panoramic views.

N.98A   7   **ST. TROPEZ**

An old town with a 16thC citadel, 18thC streets and a quaint harbour, in recent years revitalized with film star crowds, sophistication and topless sunbathing. Musée de l'Annonciade: One of the finest collections of modern painting in France, Seurat, Vlaminck, Derain, Marquet, Rouault, Matisse, Bonnard, Vuillard, Signac.

N.98
****Les Prairie de la Mer   7   **GRIMAUD**
***Les Mûres
****La Plage

Historic capital of the Maures massif; nearby Port Grimaud has been developed as a kind of miniature Venice.

***LE RANCHO

****Domaine de la   2   **ST. PONS-LES-MURES**
   Bagarède

Les Cigalons   6   **STE. MAXIME

A popular resort with four fine beaches surrounded by pine forests and mimosas.

****L'Etoile d'Argens ***St. Aygulf ***Le Provençal ***Au Paradis des Campeurs ***Le Grand Calme	16	**ST. AYGULF** There are splendid sands here and because of this St. Aygulf is rapidly growing in popularity.
****Le Colombier **Bellevue **Le Castellas **GORGE VENT	8	**FRÉJUS (Connect Route 24)** Founded in 49 BC by Julius Caesar. The amphitheatre ruins are the oldest in Gaul; there are also town gates, a theatre and town walls. Fréjus is in a charming situation between the Monts des Maures and the Esterel mountains. The old town is a mile from the sea.
****VAL-FLEURY ****L'ILE D'OR	3	**ST. RAPHAEL** A popular resort in summer and winter. The quaint old town lies around the old harbour; around the bay is the new yacht marina with fine beaches in between. Napoleon embarked for Elba from here in 1814.
****DU DRAMMONT ****ANTHEOR-PLAGE ****AGAY-SOLEIL	10	**AGAY** Most handsomely situated at the foot of the Estérel, with red rocks, blue sea and picturesque coves.
	11	**LE TRAYAS**
	3	**MIRAMAR** A resort in the midst of pines with three beaches of fine gravel.
	6	*Alpes-Maritime* **THEOULE-SUR-MER** At the end of the Esterel coast and overlooking the gulf of La Napoule, Theoule is an enchanting little place with fishing boats in the small harbour.
N.559 ****Plateau des Chasses ***Azur-Vacances ***LA FERME	13	**LA NAPOULE** Situated in a beautiful bay and linked with Mandelieu in the formation of the large yacht marina. Château de Mandelieu – La Napoule is a 14thC stronghold restored in 1919 by the American sculptor, Henry Clews, and now a Memorial Art Foundation.
N.7 ***RANCH CAMPING **BELLEVUE	11	**LA BOCCA**

84

1   **CANNES (Connect Route 24)**

One of the most fashionable resorts in the world, playground of royalty, aristocracy, the famous and the wealthy. There are splendid shops, boulevards, flowers, gardens, the largest yacht harbour in the world, casinos, festivals – there is something for everybody in this luxury resort, a most beautiful place in which just to stand and stare. Musée de la Castre: Grecian, Egyptian, Roman, Cyprian collections.

6   **GOLFE-JUAN**

Amidst orange groves in a splendid setting, the town and the shops are situated around the small harbour. It is quite a lively little place. When Napoleon returned from Elba in 1815 he landed here.

****Le Gecko

3   **JUAN-LES-PINS**

A fashionable resort with a yacht harbour and sandy beaches, linked with Antibes to make the 20 km. of the Cap d'Antibes one of the most scintillating holiday areas in the world.

****LE PYLONE
****LES MIMOSAS
****CHÂTEAU DE LA
     BRAGUE

2   **ANTIBES**

An old town, one of the oldest in France, dating back to the 5thC BC. It was a trading post in Greek times and later a fortified town; the Fort Carré on the bay

Playground of royalty . . . Cannes

**** Les Embruns
***COLOMBIA
***LOGIS DE LA BRAGUE
***Les Frênes

was built by Vauban. The old town is situated around the harbour which seems to be growing continually to accommodate more and more yachts. Antibes and Juan-les-Pins have joined forces as one holiday community. Juan is 'with it' and rather expensive whilst Antibes is more sedate as befits her age. The climate is splendid both in summer and winter and the local flower-growing industry benefits accordingly. Grimaldi Museum: The largest collection of Picasso works in one museum in existence. Terrestrial and Underwater Archaeology Museum.

****LE SOURIRE
****PARC DES MAURETTES
***L'HIPPODROME
**LE LOUBET
**ORION

8 **VILLENEUVE LOUBET**

****EUROP CAMPING
****L'OASIS
****La Rosabelle
***LE VAL FLEURI
**St. Jean
**LA RIVIÈRE
**LES NOISETIERS

4 **CAGNES-SUR-MER**
An ancient and picturesque Provençal town.
Castle Museum: Chagall, Kisling, Carzou, Seyssaud.
Maison des Colettes: Renoir's house.

****LE TODOS
***PANORAMER

1 **CROS-DE-CAGNES**

****LOU PISTOU

2 **ST. LAURENT-DU-VAR**
On the River Var, reconstructed in Provençal style and with a modern claim to fame, for the largest supermarket in France is situated by the sea here.

10 **NICE (Connect Route 31)**
Internationally famous capital of the Côte d'Azur, capital of Alpes-Maritimes, a resort with an agreeable winter climate in view of the shelter afforded by a semi-circle of hills with mountains behind. It is a bustling, prosperous, cosmopolitan city with a continuous round of fêtes and entertainments. Musée des Beaux Arts: Carpeaux, Matisse, Dufy. Musée Matisse: more than 400 canvases and drawings. Musée Masséna: Reproduction of a palace of the First Empire. Also museums of furniture, Natural History, Archaeology, Naval, Roman.

From Nice to Menton there is a choice of three roads, the Corniche Inférieure along the coast, the Moyenne Corniche above and the Grande Corniche highest of the three. With a caravan in tow the Corniche Inférieure is recommended. If proceeding from Nice direct to Italy the Grande Corniche would be preferred.

N.559

6 **VILLEFRANCHE-SUR-MER**
A picturesque port with houses rising in tiers above the beautiful bay. Chapelle St. Pierre: walls decorated with frescoes by Jean Cocteau.

4 **BEAULIEU**
A splendid and gracious resort amidst luxuriant vegetation.

Villefranche

10 **MONACO**

A principality of 350 acres within France and part of
France although it has its own money and postage
stamps. Best known for the casino of Monte Carlo
where you can try to break the bank if you are so
inclined. Millionaires' yachts grace the harbour and all
around are skyscraper apartment blocks. You are not
allowed to park your caravan in Monaco.

The changing of the guard at the palace is a colourful
ceremony that takes place just before noon every day.
Museum of Oceanography; Jardin Exotique.

Plateau St.-Michel   11 **MENTON
**St. Maurice
**Fleur de Mai   A popular winter resort because of its mild climate, in
fact so far as scenery and flowers and mild weather is
concerned Menton is the most favoured resort of the
Côte d'Azur. It is very popular with English visitors
and famous for its beauty, lemons, fêtes and August
music festival.

Boats but no caravans . . . Monaco

Route 7 BELFORT − CHAUMONT − TROYES − PARIS

MICHELIN	ROAD NO.		
MAP NO.	CARAVAN SITES	Km.	

66	**N.19** *Promenades d'Essert		*Territoire-de-Belfort* **BELFORT** On the River Savoureuse, an old town and former fortress; although mainly industrial it is quite a tourist centre from which to visit the Vosges and Jura mountains. The huge carving from the cliffs below the citadel is the Lion de Belfort. Musée des Beaux Arts: fine arts, coins, statues.
		21	*Haut-Saône* **RONCHAMP** Industral town with a church by Le Corbusier.
		12	**LURE** On the River Ognon in a wooded setting.
		33	**VESOUL (Connect Route 26)** Capital of Haut-Saône, an old town with buildings going back to the 14thC.
	***Camping-Plage	14	**PORT-SUR-SAÔNE** An elegant little place with an 18thC bridge and an 18thC church containing beautiful furnishings.
		12	**COMBEAUFONTAINE**
		25	*Haute-Marne* **FAYL-BILLOT**
	**Navarre **La Liez	25	**LANGRES (Connect Routes 5, 21)**
62		12	**ROLAMPOINT (Connect Route 21)**
	**Ste. Marie	25	**CHAUMONT (Connect Routes 18, 21)** Once the capital of Bassigny, now of Haut-Marne. It is a splendid town, rich in history. The Palace of Justice was built on the site of the castle of the Counts of Champagne, 12thC.
61	**Parc Camping de la Gravière	42	*Aube* **BAR-SUR-AUBE** An ancient town in a fine setting. Part of the 10thC defence wall is still visible. St. Pierre, 12thC; St. Maclou, 12thC.

	23	**VENDEUVRE** 17thC château.
***Municipal	31	**TROYES (Connect Route 33)** On the River Seine, once capital of Champagne and now of Aube, a city in Roman times and before. St. Pierre Cath., 12thC; St. Urbain, 12thC; St. Nizier, 15thC; Town Hall, 16thC; St. Madeleine, 16thC; Museum.
**Les Cerisiers	38	**ROMILLY-SUR-SEINE** An industrial town.
**Villiers-aux-Choix	18	**NOGENT** Pleasantly situated small town. St. Laurent, 17thC.

Seine et Marne

17 **PROVINS**

A beautiful old town with a watch-tower and town wall built by the English in the 15thC. It is the centre of a big rose-growing area. In the 13thC Edward of Lancaster, from Provins, introduced into his arms the red rose that was to triumph over the white rose of York in the Wars of the Roses. Caesar's Tower, 12thC; Porte St. Jean, 12thC; St. Quiriace, 12thC.

22 **NANGIS**

A lovely old town with a 13thC church, 16thC castle and 13thC ruined towers amongst shady boulevards.

11 **MORMANT**

8 **GUIGNES**

15 **BRIE-COMTE-ROBERT**

The old capital of the French Brie to which Robert, Count of Brie and brother of Louis VII gave his name in the 12thC. It is a thriving rose-growing centre. St. Étienne, 13thC; Castle ruins.

****BOIS-DE-BOULOGNE ****LE-TREMBLAY (*closed Jan–Feb only*) ****MAISONS-LAFFITTE INTERNATIONAL	20	**PARIS**

Route 8 BIARRITZ — PAU — TARBES — FOIX — PERPIGNAN

MICHELIN MAP NO.	ROAD NO. CARAVAN SITES	Km.	

85 | N.117
***Splendid-Camping
***Biarritz-Camping

Basses-Pyrénées
BIARRITZ (Connect Route 9)
One of the most fashionable seaside resorts in the world with a mild yet exhilarating climate. Noted for superb displays of hydrangeas in May and June. Amongst other holiday attractions are the Fireworks Display on 15 August, Festival of the Sea, bull fights, Pelota, flat racing and trotting races, luxury casinos. The Maritime Museum and Aquarium is the finest in France.

**La Chambre d'Amour
**ST. JEAN

3 **ANGLET**

****La Chêneraie

4 **BAYONNE (Connect Route 9)**
On the Rivers Nive and Adour, capital of the Basque country, an old town and commercial harbour. There are splendid shops, arcades and promenades on what were once the fortified walls of the town. Ste. Marie Cath., 12thC; Basque Museum: Folklore. Musée Bonnat: Bonnat, David, Delacroix, Ingres, Watteau. Drawings by Michelangelo, Bellini, Botticelli, Titian, Leonardo da Vinci.

35 **PEYREHORADE**

31 **ORTHEZ**

16 **LACQ**

**DU COY
**LES SAPINS
(****Municipal site in course of construction)

25 **PAU (Connect Route 35)**
Capital of the département, a town known to the Romans, with a mild climate that makes it popular as a winter resort. Château Henri IV, where Henri de Navarre was born: museum, period furniture and tapestries. Musée des Beaux Arts: paintings, engravings, numismatics.

N.637
***La Scierie
***Anclades
***Domaine de Biscaye
**THEIL

Hautes-Pyrénées
LOURDES
One of the most important places of Christian pilgrimage in the world and now host to millions of pilgrims annually. Lourdes was unknown before 1858

MICHELIN	ROAD NO.	
MAP NO.	CARAVAN SITES	Km.

**CAMP PRAT
*LE RUISSEAU BLANC

when Bernadette Soubirous revealed her visions of the Virgin. The Church of the Rosary was built (1889), alongside the Grotto. Besides the Basilica (1871), there are other churches in Lourdes including the underground Basilica St. Pius X (1958), which can accommodate 20,000 pilgrims. Castle, 13thC, above the town with Pyrenean Museum. Bernadette's house.

Created by the visions of Bernadette . . . Lourdes

MICHELIN MAP NO.	ROAD NO. CARAVAN SITES	Km.	

N. 17

Hautes-Pyrénées

82   **LES HORIZONS   39   TARBES (Connect Route 46)**

Capital of Hautes-Pyrénées, a graceful market town on the River Adour. Tarbes dates back to Roman times. It is the birthplace of Marshal Foch. Cath. 12thC; National Stud Farm; International Museum of Hussars and of the Tarbes Horse.

19   **TOURNAY**

18   **LANNEMAZAN**

Haute-Garonne

*Les Hortensias   16   **MONTREJEAU**

14   **ST. GAUDENS**

A town of boulevards and fine views amongst the old houses.

19   **ST. MARTORY**

Ariège

30   **ST. GIRONS**

86   **Lac de Labarre   44   FOIX (Connect Route 47)**

Dominated by the rock on which are the remains of the Castle of the Counts of Foix. St. Volusien, 12thC. Museum: Prehistory, Roman.

28   **LAVELANET**

Aude

35   **QUILLAN**

Pyrénées-Orientales

52   **ESTAGEL**

RELAIS SAINTONGE   22   PERPIGNAN

On the rivers Tet and Basse, an old town once the property of Spain. It is now a bustling place with many modern buildings and shops; the most fascinating part is amongst the narrow streets of the old town around the Place de la Republique. St. Jean Cath., 13thC; Castle of the Kings of Majorca, 13thC. Museums – Beaux Arts: Rigaud (born in Perpignan), David, Ingres – de Roussillon; popular arts and crafts – Natural History.

A town of wine indeed . . . Bordeaux

Route 9 BORDEAUX — BIARRITZ

MICHELIN MAP NO.	ROAD NO. CARAVAN SITES	Km.	
71	**N.10** *Municipal *LES GRAVIÈRES		*Gironde* **BORDEAUX (Connect Routes 10, 13, 22, 27, 35)** Capital of Aquitaine and fifth largest city in France, situated on the River Garonne, it was a splendid place in Roman times. Some evidence of this remains. Bordeaux is a town of industry, tourism and wine; from this port some of the finest wines in the world are shipped everywhere. St. Michel, 15thC; St. André, 12thC; St. Croix, 12thC. Museums – Maritime: ship models – Prehistoric – Natural History; Fine Arts: Botticelli, Rubens, Veronese. Botanical Gardens.
		44	**BELIN**
78	*Le Muretois	7	**LE MURET**
		25	*Landes* **LABOUHEYRE**
		42	**CASTETS**
	***Saubis	30	**ST. VINCENT-DE-TYROSSE**
	***Lou Piguada **Coy **Le Lac	20	**ONDRES**
85		5	*Basses-Pyrénées* **BAYONNE (Connect Route 8)**
	****La Chêneraie ***Splendid-Camping ***Biarritz-Camping	7	**BIARRITZ (Connect Route 8)**

Route 10 BORDEAUX – AGEN – TOULOUSE

MICHELIN MAP NO.	ROAD NO. CARAVAN SITES	Km.	
71	**N.113** *Municipal *LES GRAVIÈRES		*Gironde* **BORDEAUX (Connect Routes 9, 13, 22, 27, 35)**
		32	**PODENSAC (Connect Route 35)**
79	**Allées Marine	14	**LANGON (Connect Route 35)**
	**Le Rouergue	18	**LE REOLE** A small town above the River Garonne. Town Hall, 12thC; St. Pierre, 13thC.

Old buildings, narrow streets . . . Agen

Lot-et-Garonne

19 **MARMANDE**
An industrial town on the Garonne.

17 **TONNEINS**

Le Vieux Moulin   11 **AIGUILLON

9 **PONT-STE.-MARIE**

***MUNICIPAL   19 **AGEN**
An engaging old town with narrow streets. St. Caprais
Cath., 12thC; Notre-Dame, 13thC; Museum: Goya.

Tarn-et-Garonne
26 **VALENCE D'AGEN**

***L'Ile de Bidounet   18 **MOISSAC**
A peaceful place with a church dating back to the
7thC.

Municipal   8 **CASTELSARRASIN
St. Sauveur, 12thC; St. Jean, 15thC.

N.20
82   **Aquitaine Camping   29 **GRISOLLES (Connect Route 48)**

Haute-Garonne
***MUNICIPAL   29 **TOULOUSE (Connect Routes 46, 47, 48, 49)**
Fourth largest city in France, once capital of the
Languedoc and now of Haute-Garonne. A busy place
on the River Garonne with splendid shops, museums
and many buildings of red brick. Adam Smith wrote
The Wealth of Nations here. Jacobins, 13thC, largest
Dominican church in France. St. Sernin, 11thC., largest
and most complete Romanesque church in France;
St. Étienne Cath., 11thC; Musée des Augustins:
Boucher, Delacroix, Corot, Ingres, Poussin, Rigaud,
Rubens, Toulouse-Lautrec, also Romanesque
sculptures. Musée Paul-Dupuy: Porcelain, clocks,
musical instruments. Musée Georges Labit: Egyptian,
Oriental. Natural History.

Route 11 BREST — QUIMPER — VANNES — NANTES

MICHELIN MAP NO.	ROAD NO. CARAVAN SITES	Km.	
58	**D.33** **Ste. Anne-du-Portzic **ST. MARC		*Finistère* **BREST (Connect Route 34)** The presence of warships in the fine natural harbour shows that this is a naval town and the naval dockyard, arsenal and Admiralty Office in the castle confirm this. German warships used Brest in WW2 and huge concrete submarine pens were built here, receiving continued attention from Allied bombers that reduced the harbour to ruins. The American Forces liberated it in 1944. There is a monument commemorating American intervention in WW1. Brest is now a modern port and commercial town and a tourist centre for exploring Brittany. Naval Museum.
	N.170 **Seillou	31	**LE FAOU** An interesting little place of old houses on the Faou estuary.
	****L'Orangerie de Lanniron	46	**QUIMPER** At the confluence of the Rivers Steir and Odet, capital of Finistère, Quimper, noted for pottery and lace, is a cathedral town of historic interest dating back to Roman times. Breton influence is apparent and local costume is still worn. Cath., 12thC; Museum of Fine Arts; Breton Museum.
	N.165 ***Le Bois de Pleuven	14	**ST. YVY**
		8	**ROSPORDEN**
	***Les Genêts d'Or	11	**BANNALEC**
		15	**QUIMPERLE** A small town at the junction of the Rivers Ellé and Isole. St. Michel, 13thC; Ste. Croix, 11thC.
	D.62	12	*Morbihan* **PONT-SCORFF**
63	**D.26**	11	**HENNEBONT** An old town with ramparts on the Blavet estuary, much damaged in WW2. Notre-Dame, 16thC.

N.165	28	**AURAY** An old town noted for oyster fishing. A plaque on the quay recalls the landing here of Benjamin Franklin in 1778.
****DE CONLEAU	18	**VANNES** Capital of Morbihan, an ancient stronghold and modern tourist centre; from here you can visit the islands of the Gulf of Morbihan. St. Pierre Cath., 13thC. Archaeological Museum in the Château Gaillard where the old parliament of Brittany met over five hundred years ago.
**Municipal	25	**MUZILLAC**
**Le Pâtis	16	**LA ROCHE BERNARD**
**Le Chatellier	19	*Loire-Atlantique* **PONTCHÂTEAU**
67	48	**NANTES (Connect Routes 27, 28, 29, 45)** Capital of the département. Probably best known for the Edict of Nantes issued here in 1598 by Henry IV giving Protestants equal religious liberty with Roman Catholics. The castle in which the Edict was signed is now a museum. Nantes is a commercial centre and a seaport although thirty miles up the Loire from the Atlantic. Jules Verne was born at Nantes in 1828. Ducal Castle, 13thC; Botanical Gardens; Museum: Ingres, Botticelli, Delacroix.

The citadel in the naval town of Brest

Route 12 CHAMBÉRY – BOURG – CHALON-SUR-SAÔNE – DIJON

MICHELIN MAP NO.	ROAD NO. CARAVAN SITES	Km.	
74	N.201		*Savoie* **CHAMBÉRY (Connect Route 50)** On the River Leysse, capital of Savoie, an old town with narrow streets, Chambéry is a good centre for exploring the Savoy mountains. Many of its buildings were destroyed in WW2. St. Francis Cath., 15thC; Musée Savoisien: Antiquities, furniture, costume.
	*Camp de la Plage	28	**YENNE**
	N.504 **LAC DE BART	8	*Ain* **BELLEY** An old town situated amongst mountains. Brillat-Savarin was born here.
		26	**TENAY**
		8	**ST. RAMBERT-EN-BUGEY**
	***Les Echelles	11	**AMBERIEU-EN-BUGEY**
	N.75 **Municipal	11	**PONT D'AIN**
70	****MUNICIPAL DE CHALLES	19	**BOURG-EN-BRESSE (Connect Route 26)** Capital of Ain, a market town magnificently situated below the Jura mountains; a tourist centre also known for its own special style of furniture. The 15thC church at Brou has many outstanding features.
	***BASE DE PLEIN AIR	18	**MONTREVAL-EN-BRESSE**
		14	**ST. TRIVIER-DE-COURTS**
		14	*Saône-et-Loire* **CUISERY**
69	N.6 **Le Pas Fleury	8	**TOURNUS (Connect Route 36)** Famous for its abbey, one of the most grandiose Romanesque buildings in France. Musée Greuze: Paintings by Greuze, born here 1727.

		Km.	
		10	**SENNECY**
	****MUNICIPAL	16	**CHALON-SUR-SAÔNE (Connect Route 36)**

****MUNICIPAL   16 **CHALON-SUR-SAÔNE (Connect Route 36)**

On the River Saône, an inland port and naval dock-yard, a centre of heavy industry and of wine-growing, Chalon-sur-Saône was of importance in Roman times. Cath., 12thC; St. Pierre, 17thC. Musée Denon: Gallo-Roman collections; largest collection in France of prehistoric chipped flint implements; engravings, Vivant Denon; Chardonnet, inventor of artificial silk; Saône and inland water transport; Niepce, one of the inventors of photography, was born here 1765.

N.6
***Pâquier Fané   15 **CHAGNY (Connect Route 36)**

N.74   *Côte-d'Or*
***La Grappe d'Or   9 **MEURSAULT (Connect Route 36)**

***Les Cent Vignes   6 **BEAUNE (Connect Route 36)**

On the River Bouzaise, a pretty little town in the heart of the Burgundy vineyards, the Côte d'Or, and one-time residence of the Dukes of Burgundy. Many of the buildings date from the Middle Ages but Beaune was a place of some standing in Roman times.
Hôtel Dieu, 14thC, a hospital whose museum contains tapestries and Van der Weyden's 'Last Judgement'. The nursing nuns still wear 15thC costume.
Notre-Dame, 14thC, containing a magnificent collection of tapestries in the Tapestries Treasure House of Notre-Dame.
Museum of Wine, also museums of furniture and pictures and Burgundy handicrafts.

                16 **NUITS-ST.-GEORGES**

                3 **VOSNEE-ROMANEE**

66   ***Moulin de Vougeot   2 **VOUGEOT**

                6 **GEVREY-CHAMBERTIN**

***CAMPING DU LAC   11 **DIJON (Connect Routes 5, 18)**
***L'Orée du Bois

Route 13 CHARTRES — TOURS — POITIERS — ANGOULÊME — BORDEAUX

MICHELIN MAP NO.	ROAD NO. CARAVAN SITES	Km.
60	N.10	

Eure-et-Loire
CHARTRES (Connect Routes 29, 42)
From some way off you see the 13thC cathedral, famous throughout the world. Chartres, a market town on the River Eure, was a place of importance in Roman times. There are many picturesque old houses and churches in the Lower Town, including St. André, 12thC, and St. Pierre, 12thC. Museum: Flemish tapestries, pictures.

31   **BONNEVAL**
On the Loire, an important stronghold in the Middle Ages. There are some old buildings here, town gates, Gothic houses and the bridge over the river which is 13thC. St. Florentine abbey remains, 12thC.

Famous throughout the world, the cathedral at Chartres

		14	**CHÂTEAUDUN** Situated above the River Loire, the town was damaged in WW2, but the enormous 12thC castle, one of the most striking in France, and other historic buildings escaped destruction. La Madeleine, 12thC; St. Valérien, 12thC. Museum: Egyptology, ornithology, paintings.
	****PARC DE LOISIRS	12	**CLOYES-SUR-LE-LOIR**
	***Municipal	39	*Loir-et-Cher* **VENDÔME** Mainly an industrial town but quite an interesting tourist centre with the remains of an 11thC castle and a history dating back to pre-Roman times. La Trinité, 12thC.
64	**Parc Vauchevrier	26	*Indre-et-Loire* **CHÂTEAU-RENAULT** An industrial town mainly concerned with tanning.
	**DE L'ALOUETTE	29	**TOURS (Connect Routes 2, 4, 37)**
		12	**MONTBAZON** There are the ruins of a 12thC fortress here.
		22	**STE. MAURE-DE-TOURAINE**
68	***Bec des Deux Eaux	8	*Vienne* **PORT-DE-PILES**
		3	**LES ORMES**
		7	**DANGE**
	****Le Petit Trianon	8	**INGRANDES**
	N.10 **MUNICIPAL	8	**CHÂTELLERAULT** On the River Vienne, a manufacturing town in an agreeable situation. There is an arsenal here which has supplied the French Army for 150 years. A Descartes Museum is in the house where he lived. St. Jacques, 12thC.
		14	**LA TRICHERIE**

	**MUNICIPAL	20	**POITIERS (Connect Routes 14, 28, 41)** Capital of Vienne, the name of the town recalls the Black Prince and his defeat of King John. Five hundred years ago Parliament was here and Joan of Arc appeared before it. A most delightful town. St. Jean dates from the year 356; St. Hilaire, 11thC; Notre-Dame, 12thC; St. Pierre Cath., 12thC; Palace of Justice, 14thC.
	*Municipal	19	**VIVONNE**
	**LES PEUPLIERS	17	**COUHE**
		18	**LES MAISONS BLANCHES**
			Charente
	**Des Ormeaux	13	**RUFFEC** A small town with a 12thC church.
72	*Municipal	17	**MANSLE**
	***BOURGINES	29	**ANGOULÊME (Connect Route 5)**
		6	**LA COURONNE**
	**Muncipal	26	**BARBEZIEUX** 15thC château; St. Mathias, 11thC.
			Charente-Maritime
75		21	**CHEVANCEAUX**
			Gironde
	**LE LAC VERT	26	**CAVIGNAC**
71		14	**ST. ANDRE-DE-CUBZAC (Connect Route 27)**
71	*Municipal *LES GRAVIÈRES	24	**BORDEAUX (Connect Routes 9, 10, 22, 27, 35)**

Route 14 CHÂTEAUROUX – POITIERS – NIORT – LA ROCHELLE

MICHELIN MAP NO.	ROAD NO. CARAVAN SITES	Km.	
68	N.20 ***LE ROCHET **Les Pins		*Indre* **CHÂTEAUROUX (Connect Route 48)** Capital of Indre. There is here an imposing castle and a 13thC church but the town is mainly industrial. 10 km. on N.725, at Diors, is the Museum of Three Wars. Small museum: Napoleonic items.
	N.151	30	**ST. GAULTIER (Connect Route 41)**
	N.727	29	**LE BLANC** On the River Creuse, a market town with a castle. St. Genitour, 12thC; St. Étienne, 17thC.

The British have defended and attacked . . . La Rochelle

N.151		*Vienne*
	18	**ST. SAVIN**
***LA FONTAINE	19	**CHAUVIGNY**

On the River Vienne, overlooked by several castle ruins. St. Pierre, 12thC; Notre-Dame, 11thC.

**MUNICIPAL	23	**POITIERS (Connect Routes 13, 28, 41)**
N.10		
N.11		
**De Vauchiron	25	**LUSIGNAN**
		Deux-Sèvres
**Le Panier-Fleuri	25	**ST. MAIXENT-L'ECOLE**

An ancient town with the ruins of an abbey and a castle.

71   *Municipal   23   **NIORT (Connect Route 27)**

Capital of Deux-Sèvres, with a castle, much industry and a pleasant situation on the River Sèvres.

	10	**FRONTENAY-ROHAN-ROHAN**
	13	**MAUZE-S-LE-MIGNON**
N.22		*Charente-Maritime*
***PORT NEUF	40	**LA ROCHELLE**

An old seaport that was once a rich trading centre. Champlain sailed from here to colonize Canada. Most pictures of La Rochelle include the towers and battlements in which the Rochelais and British once fought side-by-side against the French; on other occasions a chain was drawn across the harbour entrance from the Tour de la Chaine to keep the British out. This chain can still be seen, by the Musée d'Orbigny. There are splendid parks and a fascinating harbour. Town Hall, 12thC; St. Louis Cath., 17thC. Musée Lafaille: Natural History. Botanical Garden.

MICHELIN MAP NO.	ROAD NO. CARAVAN SITES	Km.	
54	N.13 **MUNICIPAL		*Manche* **CHERBOURG** An important seaport, naval base and popular ferry terminal to England. During WW2 Cherbourg was the receiving end of PLUTO, the petrol supply pipe laid underwater from the Isle of Wight. A town with an interesting shipping and yacht harbour. Thomas Henry Museum: Fra Angelico, Murillo, Van Dyck, David, Chardin, Millet; Natural History Museum; War and Liberation Museum.
	*Municipal	20	**VALOGNES** A pretty market town, former capital of the Cotentin, completely rebuilt after the devastation of 1944. Museum of shells, fossils etc., also a Cider Museum.
		7	**MONTEBOURG**
		10	**STE.-MÈRE-ÉGLISE**

Part of the harbour . . . Cherbourg

| | ***Le Haut-Dyk | 13 | **CARENTAN** |

CARENTAN
A market town and distribution centre for Normandy butter. Featured prominently in WW2, being captured by an American Airborne Division. Notre-Dame, 12thC; War Museum.

Calvados

| | **MUNICIPAL | 11 | **ISIGNY** |

| | ***MUNICIPAL | 33 | **BAYEUX** |

BAYEUX
World-famous for the Bayeux Tapestry. This is 235 ft. long by 20 in. wide and is an embroidered historical document almost 900 years old. Queen Mathilde is supposed to have made it, in 58 scenes or panels, illustrating the conquest of England by her husband William. Other learned opinion takes the view that it was made in England. The tapestry is in a glass case in a house or small museum by the cathedral. Apart from the tapestry there is a great deal of historical interest in Bayeux for it is a very old town recalling William the Conqueror and the Hundred Years War. It was an important place in Roman times and in 1944, when it featured prominently in the Normandy landings. Surprisingly it was not damaged in WW2. Bayeux is also noted for the manufacture of porcelain and lace. Notre-Dame Cath., 11thC; Botanical Gardens; British War Cemetery; Invasion Museum with the remains of Mulberry Harbour is nearby.

| | | 27 | **CAEN** |

CAEN
On the River Orne, capital of Calvados and a cultural and artistic centre. Caen is virtually a new town for much of it was destroyed in WW2, although some ancient monuments survived and others have been rebuilt in painstaking fashion. St. Pierre, 13thC; La Trinitié and St. Étienne, both founded 11thC.

| *55* | **Municipal | 51 | **LISIEUX** |

LISIEUX
Amidst delightful country on the banks of the rivers Touques and Orbiquet. Known throughout the English-speaking world for the Little Flower (Ste.-Thérèse de l'Enfant-Jésus), who died in 1897 at the age of 24 having achieved fame through *The Story of a Soul* and whose grave became a place of pilgrimage second only to Lourdes. Carmelite Convent Church contains a shrine. In 1925 Pope Pius XI canonized Thérèse and initiated the foundation of the Basilica.

Eure

★★Municipal   72   **EVREUX (Connect Route 42)**
Capital of Eure, a market town dating back to pre-Roman times. Considerably damaged in WW2. Notre-Dame Cath., 12thC; Bishop's Palace, 14thC; Museum.

17   **PACY-SUR-EURE**
A small town with a 12thC Gothic church.

A.13

Seine-et-Oise

24   **MANTES**
William the Conqueror fell from his horse at the capture of Mantes in 1087, receiving the injury from which he died. Notre-Dame, 12thC. A charming town on the River Seine rebuilt after WW2 damage.

25   **ST. GERMAIN**
On the Seine. Kings of France built castles here.

A.13

16   **VERSAILLES**
Capital of Seine-et-Oise and capital of France for a hundred years during the reigns of Louis XIV, Louis XV and Louis XVI. Several tours of the enormous palace are necessary to appreciate its glories. It has suffered much neglect and much restoration since the time of Louis XIV. The ghosts of history are everywhere; Louis XV; Louis XVI and Marie Antoinette; the Paris mob and the Revolution; the proclamation of the German Empire in 1871; the Treaty of Versailles (another), in 1919. Château of Versailles and the Trianons; History Museum.
There is a Museum of Photography in the Town Hall at nearby Bièvres (from Versailles along N.186 in the A.6 direction, turn right on N.306 past the Centre Technique Citroën). In the museum are early cameras from Daguerre on and forerunners of Ermanox, Contessa, Nettel, Leica, Contaflex and Rolleiflex plus oil darkroom lamps and early accessories.

★★★★BOIS-DE-BOULOGNE   10   **PARIS**
(*closed Jan–Feb only*)
★★★★LE-TREMBLAY
★★★★MAISONS-LAFFITTE
INTERNATIONAL

MICHELIN MAP NO.	ROAD NO. CARAVAN SITES	Km.	
73	**N.9**		*Puy-de-Dôme* **CLERMONT-FERRAND (Connect Routes 22, 25, 38)** One-time capital of Auvergne and now of Puy-de-Dôme, it is a big industrial town, a world centre of the rubber industry, also a centre of tourism and a source of mineral springs. The town is built on an extinct volcano and the cathedral is of black lava stone. On the Sunday following 15 May there is a procession around the former precincts of the town, attended by more than 100,000 people in the Pilgrimage of Notre-Dame-du-Port. Notre-Dame Cath., 13thC. Musée Bargoin: prehistoric and Gallo-Roman. Musée de Ranquet: local history and art. Musée Lecoq: natural science.
		35	**ISSOIRE (Connect Route 25)** An old fortified town, but boulevards have replaced the ramparts; a maze of narrow streets remains. It is the largest centre in France for the rolling of light alloys. International Gliding Centre.
		10	**ST. GERMAIN LEMBRON (Connect Route 25)** An ancient Gallo-Roman settlement, fortified in the 15thC.
76	****Européen**	9	*Haute-Loire* **LEMPDES (Connect Route 25)**
	N.102	15	**BRIOUDE** A market town noted for salmon fishing. St. Michael, 13thC.
	**Bouthezard	65	**LE PUY** Capital of the département, it is a famous lace-making centre; old women make lace at their doorsteps in the narrow streets. Rocher St. Michel, a striking statue of the Virgin. Crozatier Museum: collection of lace, enamels, pictures.
	N.88 **N.102**	62	*Ardèche* **MAYRES**
	**Pont de Mercier	7	**THUEYTS**

	***LES PINS	20	**AUBENAS** In a high position overlooking the River Ardèche.
80	****Le Pommier	15	**VILLENEUVE-DE-BERG**
	**Municipal	25	**VIVIERS (Connect Route 32)**
81	**N.86** **N.7**	7	**DONZÈRE**
		24	*Vaucluse* **MONDRAGON**
	**St. Eutrope	15	**ORANGE (Connect Route 36)** On the River Meyne, well known for its Roman remains including the celebrated Theatre built in the first century AD. The outer wall, 338 ft. across by 125 ft. high, Louis XIV called 'the finest wall in my kingdom'. The Triumphal Arch commemorates Caesar's victory in 49 BC. The name of the ruling house of Holland originated here.
80	****MUNICIPAL ***BAGATELLE	29	**AVIGNON (Connect Routes 6, 30, 36)**

Palace of the Popes . . . Avignon

Route 17 DUNKIRK — CALAIS — BOULOGNE —
ABBEVILLE — BEAUVAIS — PARIS

MICHELIN MAP NO.	ROAD NO. CARAVAN SITES	Km.	

51   **N.40**
    ***MUNICIPAL

Nord

DUNKIRK
Probably best known for the evacuation of the British
Army in 1940 at which time much of the town was
destroyed. It had been considerably damaged in WW1
and destroyed about 250 years previously by the
Dutch. Now it is a modern seaport and fishing port
with splendid beaches. Museum: Dunkirk Memorial
to British soldiers.

18   **GRAVELINES**

Pas-de-Calais

***MUNICIPAL   22   **CALAIS**
Was almost completely destroyed in WW2 and is
therefore a comparatively modern town. It is mainly a
cross-channel terminal, being the nearest French port
to England; its fine beaches make it a popular holiday
resort.

N.1   20   **MARQUISE**
Noted for marble quarries.

***LE MOULIN WILBERT   14   **BOULOGNE-SUR-MER**
A principal seaport at the mouth of the River Liane, a
popular seaside resort and fishing harbour noted for
herrings. Much of the lower town has been rebuilt
since WW2. The cathedral is within the massive walls
of the upper town.
Museum: Egyptian, vases.

15   **SAMER**

22   **MONTREUIL**
Was a port in Roman times and a flourishing town in
the Middle Ages when it was destroyed. Most of
Montreuil dates from the 17thC, but WW1 and WW2
took their toll.

52   **RENDEZ-VOUS
    DES CAMPERS
*RELAIS DU PONTHIEU

Somme

44   **ABBEVILLE (Connect Route 1)**

8   **PONT-RÉMY**

12 **AIRAINES**
An old town with many churches and a ruined castle.
Notre-Dame, 12thC; Priory, 12thC; St. Denis, 15thC.

22 **POIX**
A pleasantly situated little place with a striking Gothic
church, 16thC.

Amiens cathedral, largest in France

N.29
***L'ETANG ST. PIERRE   26 **AMIENS**

A city of many canals on the River Somme. Capital of
Somme, once of Picardy, an established town in
Roman times. H.Q. of the British Army in WW1 and
nearly destroyed in WW2. A manufacturing town
specializing in velvet. The largest Gothic cathedral in
France is here. Notre-Dame, 13thC. Musée de
Picardie: Boucher, Fragonard, La Tour, Chardin,
Delacroix, Bonnard, Matisse, Gauguin. Water market:
fruit and vegetables sold from punts at quayside near
Place Parmentier, Tuesday, Thursday and Saturday.
Zoo.

55   **N.1**

Oise

15 **GRANDVILLIERS**

MUNICIPAL   29 **BEAUVAIS (Connect Route 44)

On the River Thérain. The 13thC cathedral of St.
Pierre was spared from the destruction of the rest of
the town, including the famous tapestry factory, in
WW2. In the cathedral is the largest astronomical
clock in the world, also remarkable windows and
tapestries. It was a bishop of Beauvais (Cauchon), who
passed sentence on Joan of Arc at Rouen. Five
hundred years later, on 5 October 1930, Beauvais
featured tragically in the world's headlines when the
British airship R.101, in flight to India, crashed and
burst into flames there with the loss of 48 lives.
St. Pierre Cath., 12thC, has the highest vaulting in the
world. St. Étienne, 12thC. Musée Départemental:
Prehistoric, Gallo-Roman, wood carvings, lapidary,
ceramics, stoneware, tapestries.

56

15 **NOAILLES**

49 **ST. DENIS (Connect Route 20)**
An industrial suburb of Paris.

****BOIS-DE-BOULOGNE   9 **PARIS**
  (*Closed Jan–Feb only*)
****LE-TREMBLAY
****MAISONS-LAFFITTE
  INTERNATIONAL

Route 18 GENEVA (Switzerland) – DIJON – CHAUMONT

MICHELIN MAP NO.	ROAD NO. CARAVAN SITES	Km.	
	N.5		*Switzerland* **GENEVA (Connect Route 50)**
70			*France* *Jura*
		5	**FERNEY-VOLTAIRE**
		11	**GEX**
		30	**LES ROUSSES** A tourist and winter sports resort being developed, with ski-lifts, at the foot of Noirmont.
		10	**MOREZ**
	*Municipal	3	**MORBIER**
	**Champ de Mars	13	**ST. LAURENT-EN-GRANDVAUX** A commercial town principally engaged in cheese-making. Not very attractive.
	***De Boyse	23	**CHAMPAGNOLE** On the River Ain, with an 18thC church and castle ruins, in beautiful wooded surroundings in the centre of the Jura. There are factories here but also, nearby, the pine forest of La joux, one of the most beautiful in France.
		23	**POLIGNY (Connect Route 26)** By the River Orain. St. Hippolyte, 15thC; Hôtel-Dieu, 17thC.
	***Les Bords de Loue	29	**PARCEY**
70 *66*	**L'ILE DU PASQUIER	9	**DOLE** An industrial town in an attractive setting on the River Doubs. In the old part of the town there are steep narrow streets. Louis Pasteur was born here (1822), and his house is now a museum. Notre-Dame, 16thC.
	N.5 **L'Arquebuse	18	*Côte d'Or* **AUXONNE** An old military town where Lieutenant Bonaparte was garrisoned prior to the Revolution. Museum commemorates this.

		14	**GENLIS**
	***CAMPING DU LAC ***L'Oree du Bold	20	**DIJON (Connect Routes 5, 12)**
	N.71 **Municipal	24	**ST. SEINE L'ABBAYE**
	*Municipal	13	**CHANCEAUX** Near the source of the Seine (a 100-year-old rural park), to which pilgrimages were made in Gallo-Roman times. 15thC houses. In the broad main street are parked old coaches and post-chaises.
65	**MUNICIPAL	46	**CHÂTILLON-SUR-SEINE** An agreeable little town that has been largely rebuilt following damage in WW2. St. Vorles, 11thC; Museum: Archaeological collections.
	N.65		*Haute-Marne*
		36	**CHÂTEAUVILLAIN**
62	**Ste. Marie	21	**CHAUMONT (Connect Routes 7, 21)**

Route 19 LE HAVRE – ROUEN (Via N.13Bis)

MICHELIN MAP NO.	ROAD NO. CARAVAN SITES	Km.	
52	**N.13 Bis**		*Seine-Maritime*
55	★★Municipal		**LE HAVRE**
			On the River Seine. Practically all the town is new since Le Havre was destroyed in WW2. It is principally a port with nearly ten miles of quays, also a cross-Channel terminal of growing importance. St. Joseph's church is built of reinforced concrete.
		7	**HARFLEUR**
			An industrial suburb of Le Havre. Henry V landed here before Agincourt.
		9	**ST. ROMAIN**
		11	**BOLBEC**
			An industrial town.
		22	**YVETOT**
			Many of the buildings are modern following WW2 destruction. Museum: Carved ivory.
		19	**BARENTAN**
		11	**MAROMME**
	★★ROUEN BONSECOURS	6	**ROUEN (Connect Routes 1, 42, 43, 44)**

Rebuilt after war destruction . . . Le Havre

Route 20 LILLE – ARRAS – PARIS (AUTOROUTE)

MICHELIN MAP NO.	ROAD NO. CARAVAN SITES	Km.	
51	**A.1**		*Nord*
			LILLE (Connect Route 21)
			On the canalized River Deule, capital of Nord, a bustling industrial town mainly famous for cotton-spinning (thus Lisle thread). General de Gaulle was born here. The International Fair is an attraction in May. St. Maurice, 14thC; Town Gateways, 16thC; Musée des Beaux Arts: Botticelli, El Greco, Goya, Frans Hals, Holbein, Jordaens, Rubens, Tintoretto, Van Dyck, Veronese, David, Monet, Sisley, Renoir.
	**DE LEU PINDU	21	**LE NEUVILLE** (Autoroute Junction at CARVIN)
			Pas de Calais
		41	**ARRAS** On the River Scarpe, capital of Pas de Calais, an ancient city of gabled houses and squares with arcades, known for cloth-making since Roman times and famous for tapestry. War damage has been restored, including Town Hall, originally 1460, and Cathedral. There are many military cemeteries and memorials here.
			Somme
		72	**ROYE** An industrial town.
56	***CHÂTEAU DE SOREL	21	*Oise* **ORVILLERS-SOREL** (Autoroute Junction at **Ressons-sur-Matz**)
		38	**SENLIS** One of the best-preserved old towns in France, with narrow streets and Roman remains. Once a residence of the Kings of France. Château Royal – museum of hunting. Notre-Dame Cath., 12thC.
		39	**St. DENIS (Connect Route 17)**
	****BOIS-DE-BOULOGNE (*Closed Jan–Feb only*) ****LE-TREMBLAY ****MAISONS-LAFFITTE INTERNATIONAL	9	**PARIS**

Route 21 LILLE – CAMBRAI – LAON – REIMS – CHÂLONS-SUR-MARNE – CHAUMONT – BESANÇON

MICHELIN MAP NO.	ROAD NO. CARAVAN SITES	Km.	
51	**A.1**		*Nord* **LILLE (Connect Route 20)**
	N.43	40	**DOUAI** On the Scarpe canal, an old town in a coal-mining area, much damaged in WW1 and WW2. Town Hall, 15thC.
53	**N.17** ***PARC DE PLEIN-AIR	12	**BRUNEMONT**
	***MODERNE	2	**AUBIGNY-AU-BAC**
		11	**CAMBRAI** A manufacturing town, mainly textiles and linen (thus 'cambric' linen). Damaged in both wars; in WW1 the Battle of Cambrai saw the introduction of tanks.
	N.44 Bis	13	**HONNECOURT-S-ESCAUT**
		24	*Aisne* **ST. QUENTIN** On the River Somme, an industrial town, mainly producing textiles. A prominent battle area in WW1. St. Quentin, 12thC; Town Hall, 14th C. Museum: Entomology (insects).
	N.44	23	**LA FÈRE** There is an excellent museum here with Flemish paintings, etc.
	**Municipal	22	**LAON (Connect Route 23)** Capital of Aisne. The old town is on a hill crowned by its magnificent cathedral. The newer town is below, linked by steep, winding slopes, 265 steps and a rack-rail tramway. Notre-Dame Cath., 12thC; St. Martin, 12thC.
56	**Les Grevières	30	**BERRY-AU-BAC**

Many kings were crowned here . . . Reims cathedral

Marne

★★★Camp de Champagne	20	**REIMS (RHEIMS) (Connect Route 44)**

On the River Vesle, a capital in Celtic times. Many kings of France were crowned in the magnificent Gothic cathedral which is famous all over the world (13thC, damaged WW1 and restored). Outside is a statue of Joan of Arc who attended the coronation here of Charles VII.

Reims is in the centre of the champagne country and visits can be made to the underground cellars where millions of bottles of champagne are maturing in galleries hundreds of miles long and where you can watch the preparation of champagne.

The German surrender in France in WW2 was signed at Reims and the War Room, in its original state, can be seen. There are many picturesque and colourful markets. St. Remi, 11thC. Musée St. Denis: Bonnard, Corot, David, Delacroix, Dufy, Gauguin, Latour, Matisse, Millet, Monet, Picasso, Pissarro, Poussin, Renoir. Tau Museum: Treasures of the crownings of the Kings of France.

	8	**VAL-DE-VESLE**

★★★★Municipal	35	**CHÂLONS-SUR-MARNE**

Capital of Marne, on the River Marne, a commercial town of great age in the champagne country; a picturesque place of gardens. Damaged in WW1 and WW2. St. Étienne Cath., 13thC; St. Alpin, 12thC; Notre-Dame, 12thC; St. Loup, 15thC. Museum: Prehistoric, Gallo-Roman.

61	31	**VITRY-LE-FRANÇOIS (Connect Route 39)**

On the rivers Marne and Saulx and several canals. Notre-Dame, 17thC.

N.4 ★★★★LES CHARMILLES	11	**THIEBLEMONT-FAREMONT (Connect Route 39)**

Haute-Marne

★★Municipal	18	**ST. DIZIER (Connect Route 39)**

An industrial town. St. Martin, 13thC.

N.67	11	**EURVILLE**

66	★★Le Petit Bois	21	**JOINVILLE (Connect Route 33)**

An attractive small town above the River Marne. Notre-Dame, 12thC.

		23	**VIGNORY** 11thC pre-Romanesque priory church.
62	****Ste. Marie**	19	**CHAUMONT (Connect Routes 7, 18)**
	N.19	25	**ROLAMPOINT (Connect Route 7)**
66	****Navarre** ****La Lez**	13	**LANGRES (Connect Routes 5, 7)**
	N.67	10	**LONGEAU (Connect Route 5)**

Haute-Saône

23 **CHAMPLITTE-ET-LE-PRELOT**

A picturesque fortified town with wine-growers' houses, convents, 16thC mansions and a castle.

61	*****Longue-Rive**	19	**GRAY**

An elegant little market town on the River Saône.

66		25	**MARNAY**

Doubs

	La Plage ****Chalezeule	21	**BESANÇON (Connect Route 26)**

On the River Doubs, overlooked by the massive citadel built by Vauban in the 17thC, Besançon is capital of the Doubs département of Franche-Comté and was a capital in Roman times. It is a holiday resort and excellent touring centre from which to explore the Jura mountains; a centre of clock-making and silk production. Victor Hugo was born here, also the Lumière brothers. Pernod is made here. St. Jean Cath., 12thC. Musée des Beaux Arts: Courbet, Boucher, David, Fragonard. Watches and clocks. Citadelle Vauban, originally occupied by a Gallo-Roman city. Porte Noire, triumphal arch built 2ndC AD to glory of Marcus Aurelius.

Route 22 LYON – CLERMONT-FERRAND – BRIVE – PÉRIGUEUX – BORDEAUX

MICHELIN MAP NO.	CARAVAN SITES	Km.
74	**N.89**	
73	****PORTE DE LYON	

Rhône

LYON (Connect Routes 26, 36, 41)

At the junction of the Rhône and Saône, Lyon is a gracious city, the third largest in France, capital of the Rhône département and European capital of the silk industry, with a history going back to Roman times. Although there is a great deal of industry here, mainly textiles, it does not intrude. There is a zoo and what is claimed to be the largest rose garden in the world with 100,000 roses on permanent display. Notre-Dame de Fourvière, 19thC, reached by funicular railway. Many museums – Beaux Arts: Claude, David, Delacroix, Gauguin, Manet, Renoir. Historique des Tissus: decoration of cloth. International de la Marionnette: puppet museum. Natural History.

Hôtel de Ville, Lyon

6	**CRAPONNE**
22	**YZERON**
12	**DUERNE**
6	**STE. FOY L'ARGENTIÈRE**

Loire
23	**FEURS (Connect Route 32)**
18	**BOEN**
27	**NOIRTABLE**

Puy-de-Dôme
25	**THIERS**

Principal town in France for the manufacture of cutlery. Thiers has a long history for the Celts once occupied the site. Situated on the River Drolle it is a quaint town of narrow streets lined with 15thC houses. St. Genès, 11thC. Museum: Display of cutlery.

5	**PONT-DE-DORE**
11	**LEZOUX**

An important pottery-making centre in Gallo-Roman times. The remains of 160 potters' ovens have been unearthed. Archaeological Museum.

13	**PONT-DU-CHÂTEAUX**
15	**CLERMONT-FERRAND (Connect Routes 16, 25, 38)**

***CLERMONT–CEYRAT	6	**CEYRAT**
	19	**ROCHEFORT-MONTAGUE**
	25	**BOURG-LASTIC**

Delightfully situated amidst pine forests. Nearby is the reservoir lake of Bort, largest in Europe.

Corrèze
9	**EYGURANDE**
21	**USSEL**

A fascinating little town with a number of interesting buildings and a 6 ft. high granite Roman eagle.

		Km.	
		29	**EGLETONS**
		32	**TULLE** A handsome town with an interesting 12thC cathedral.
	***LA FERME DES ILES	28	**BRIVE-LA-GAILLARDE (Connect Route 48)** On the River Corrèze, a market town in lovely surroundings. St. Martin, 11thC.
		20	*Dordogne* **TERRASON**
		21	**THENON**
75	***BARNABE-PLAGE ***L'Isle	34	**PÉRIGUEUX** On the River Isle, capital of Dordogne, a town with Gallic origins now noted for truffles and pâtés de foie gras, for sale at many roadsides. St. Front Cath., 12thC; Roman remains; Périgord Museum.

From Périgueux on RN.710 and D.47 it is a short distance to the National Museum of Prehistory at Les Eyzies, said to be the world's capital of Prehistory in view of the antiquities unearthed there. There are the magnificent caves of Lascaux, Font de Gaume, Les Combarelles and Cap Blanc with wall paintings, engravings etc. In July and August excursions are organized from Périgueux accompanied by a lecturer from the Caisse National des Monuments Historique.

		Km.	
75	**N.89**	38	**MUSSIDAN** An industrial town on the River Isle.
		17	**MONTPON**
	***Camp du Ruste	29	*Gironde* **LIBOURNE** At the junction of the rivers Dordogne and Isle, Libourne is accessible to seagoing ships. Wine is exported from here. St. Jean, 15thC.
	*Municipal *LES GRAVIÈRES	32	**BORDEAUX (Connect Routes 9, 10, 13, 27, 35)**

Route 23 MAUBEUGE – LAON – SOISSONS – PARIS

MICHELIN MAP NO.	ROAD NO. CARAVAN SITES	Km.	
53	N.2 *MUNICIPAL		*Nord* **MAUBEUGE** An industrial town with splendid gardens; the considerable damage of WW2 has been made good so that Maubeuge is now modern. Zoo.
	****Château de Dourlers	12	**DOURLERS**
	*Champ de Mars	6	**AVESNES-S-HELPE**
		18	*Aisne* **LA CAPELLE**
	**Val d'Oise	8	**ETREAUPONT**
	**Municipal	58	**LAON (Connect Route 21)**
56	**Municipal		**SOISSONS (Connect Route 44)** An important place in Gallo-Roman times, now quite a pleasant town on the River Aisne although mainly industrial. Damaged in both wars. In the 12thC cathedral is Rubens's 'Adoration of the Shepherds'. St. Léger, 13thC; St. Jean, 13thC, noted for its association with Thomas Becket.
		24	**VILLER-COTTERETS** There is a splendid Renaissance château here at the edge of the forest that was one of the great royal hunting-grounds.
		25	*Seine-et-Marne* **NANTEUIL-LE-HAUDOUIN**
		15	**DAMMARTIN-EN-GOELE** A small city, ancient capital of the Pays de Goele, looking out over fields and orchards. Notre-Dame, 13thC.
	****BOIS-DE-BOULOGNE (*Closed Jan–Feb only*) ****LE-TREMBLAY ****MAISONS-LAFFITTE INTERNATIONAL	30	**PARIS**

Route 24 MONTPELLIER – ARLES – AIX-EN-PROVENCE – CANNES

MICHELIN MAP NO.	ROAD NO. CARAVAN SITES	Km.	
83	N.113		*Hérault* **MONTPELLIER (Connect Routes 25, 30)** City of art with narrow picturesque streets dating from the Middle Ages, on the River Merdanson 10 km. from the Mediterranean; above the imposing town is an Arc de Triomphe (1691), at one end and a castle, Château d'Eau (18thC), at the other. St. Pierre Cath., 14thC; Botanical Garden; Musée Fabre: Courbet, Delacroix, Matisse.
		21	**LUNEL (Connect Route 30)**
	N.572	10	**AIMARGUES**
		22	*Bouches-du-Rhône* **ST. GILLES**
	**Les Rosiers	19	**ARLES** An ancient town on the River Rhône, a capital in Roman times, with many important Roman and medieval buildings, Roman theatre, amphitheatre, Alyscamps (cemetery) and necropolis. The forum, on the site of the Roman forum, is still the town centre. Two storeys of the amphitheatre, with sixty arches each, are fairly well preserved. Little remains of the Roman theatre, built in the time of Augustus. The church, once cathedral, of St. Trophime, is said to have been founded in 606. With the most southerly bridge over the Rhône forming a link between Italy and Spain, Arles is situated where the Rhône divides into two channels bounding the Camargue. Traffic jams here are considerable. Bull-fights. Museums: Roman and pagan art; also Picasso, Matisse, Gauguin, Utrillo.
	N.113 ***La Crau	17	**ST. MARTIN-DE-CRAU**
84	**NOSTRADAMUS	24	**SALON DE PROVENCE (Connect Route 6)**
	N.572 **INTERNATIONAL CAMPING	18	**ST. CANNAT**

N.7
****ARC-EN-CIEL
****CHANTECLER
***FELIBRIGE

17 **AIX-EN-PROVENCE**
A fine city, spa and health resort, capital of the Counts
of Provence in the 12thC. Tree-lined promenades,
splendid shops and fine old houses. Birthplace of
Cézanne and early home of Zola. The thermal springs
here were used by the Romans. St. Marie Madeleine,
1440; St. Jean-de-Malte, 13thC; St. Sauveur Cath.,
12thC. (the Flemish tapestries were once in
Canterbury Cathedral). Town Hall, 16thC, with
Méjanes Library, one of the most splendid in France
(Book of Hours illustrated by King René).
Archbishop's Palace; museum of tapestry. Pavilion
Cézanne; Musée Granet: paintings, sculpture.
International Festival of Music, 10–31 July.

Var

39 **ST. MAXIMIN-LA-STE. BAUME**
A small town named after Maximinus, martyred
bishop of Aix who is buried here. So, it is said, is
Mary Magdalen.

33 **BRIGNOLES**
An industrial town with a lovely church, St. Sauveur.

24 **LE LUC**

**Le Relax

23 **LE MUY**

****DES AUBREDES
***Les Hautes-Vernèdes

11 **PUGET-SUR-ARGENS**

****Le Colombier
**Bellevue
**Le Castellas
**GORGE-VENT

5 **FREJUS (Connect Route 6)**

Alpes-Maritime

****Plateau des Chasses
***Les Cigales
***Les Cerisiers
***Le Roc Fleuri
***LES PRUNIERS
***Azur

29 **MANDELIEU**

7 **CANNES (Connect Route 6)**

Route 25 MONTPELLIER — MILLAU — ST.-FLOUR — CLERMONT-FERRAND

MICHELIN MAP NO.	ROAD NO. CARAVAN SITES	Km.	
83	N.109		*Hérault* **MONTPELLIER (Connect Routes 24, 30)**
	**DU PONT	30	**GIGNAC**
		4	**ST. ANDRÉ-DE-SAGONIS**
	N.9	20	**LODÈVE** A quaint old town on the River Soulondres. St. Fulcran Cath., 13thC.
	*Roc Castel	20	**LE CAYLAR**
80		22	*Avreyon* **LA CAVALERIE**

Old buildings, picturesque streets . . . Montpellier

		Km.	
	****Millau-Plage **Graufesenque **Millau-Cureplat	19	**MILLAU** Regional capital on the rivers Tarn and Dourbie, a commercial town, centre of the glove-making industry. The old houses are attractive, also the covered arcades around the Place Foch. Notre-Dame, 12thC. Musée de la Ganterie: History of glove-making. Musée Gallo-Roman. Nearby are the canyons of the Tarn and Jonte, the Château Sambucy and the caves of Roquefort in which the cheese is made.
		32	**SEVERAC-LE-CHÂTEAU**
			Lozère
		20	**BANASSAC**
		21	**CHIRAC**
		4	**MARVEJOLS** A small market town with 14thC fortified gateways and an ancient fortress.
		21	**AUMONT-AUBRAC**
76	*Municipal	10	**ST. CHELY-D'APCHER**
			Cantal
	***Des Orgues **Du Lander	34	**ST.-FLOUR (Connect Route 46)** The houses seem to be climbing up the green hill, at the top of which stands the massive 15thC cathedral with a remarkable 15thC Christ in black wood. Museum: Religious art.
	***L'Allagnon	31	**MASSIAC** In the beautiful Allagon valley, a small town with traces of its former ramparts. St. Madeleine, 12thC.
			Haute-Loire
	**Européen	24	**LEMPDES (Connect Route 16)**
			Puy-de-Dôme
73		9	**ST. GERMAIN-LEMBRON (Connect Route 16)**
		10	**ISSOIRE (Connect Route 16)**
		35	**CLERMONT-FERRAND (Connect Routes 16, 22, 38)**

Route 26 NANCY – EPINAL – BESANÇON – BOURG – LYON

MICHELIN MAP NO.	ROAD NO. CARAVAN SITES	Km.	
62	N.57 ***DE BRABOIS		*Meurthe-et-Moselle* **NANCY (Connect Routes 5, 33, 39)**
			Vosges
		45	**CHARMES**
		18	**THAON-LES-VOSGES**
	**Le Château	10	**EPINAL** On the River Moselle, an industrial town with parks and gardens by the river. St. Maurice, 13thC. Castle ruins.
	**La Demoiselle **Charade	28	**REMIREMONT** On the River Moselle in a charming situation with many interesting old buildings.
	**L'Hermitage	14	**PLOMBIERS-LES-BAINS** A well-known spa amongst woods whose mineral waters were appreciated in Roman times.
			Haute-Saône
		12	**FOUGEROLLES** In the beautiful valley of Combeauté; it is a centre for the distilling of Kirsch liqueur.
	**MUNICIPAL	9	**LUXEUIL-LES-BAINS** A well-known spa in a delightful wooded situation.
		17	**SAULX**
66		14	**VESOUL (Connect Route 7)**
	*Municipal	25	**RIOZ**
	**La Plage **Chalezeule	27	*Doubs* **BESANÇON (Connect Route 21)**
70	N.83	18	**QUINGEY** On the River Loue, with ruins of an ancient feudal castle.

Jura

LA HALTE JURASSIENNE   17   **MOUCHARD
Amidst the forests of Fresse. National School of
Wood.

***Municipal   9   **ARBOIS**
A picturesque small town surrounded by vineyards.
Pasteur lived here as a boy (he was born at Dole), and
the Musée de la Maison Paternelle de Pasteur contains
exhibits of his life. Tour de la Gloriette, 13thC,
remains of ramparts, 17thC houses with arcades.

                                11   **POLIGNY (Connect Route 18)**

Du Miel   18   **ST. GERMAIN-LES-ARLAY

Municipal   12   **LONS-LE-SAUNIER
On the River Vallière, a prettily situated spa and
holiday resort. It is also an industrial town specializing
in the manufacture of cheese, clocks, spectacles, toys
and chocolate. Rouget-de-Lisle was born here. St.
Desiré, 11thC. Musée Municipal: Prehistory, also
Courbet, Breughel, Largillière.

                                15   **BEAUFORT**

                                11   **CUISEAUX**

MUNICIPAL   7   **ST. AMOUR
An agreeable holiday resort with nearby marble
quarries.

Ain
                                7   **COLIGNY**

***Le Sevron   11   **ST. ETIENNE-DU-BOS**

****MUNICIPAL DE CHALLES   12   **BOURG-EN-BRESSE (Connect Route 12)**

74   ****Les Autières   29   **VILLARS-LES-DOMBES**

73   *Rhône*

74   ****PORTE DU LYON   34   **LYON (Connect Routes 22, 36, 41)**

Route 27 NANTES – NIORT – BORDEAUX

MICHELIN MAP NO.	ROAD NO. CARAVAN SITES	Km.	
67	N.137		*Loire-Atlantique* **NANTES (Connect Routes 11, 28, 29, 45)**
	**Les Vallées Fleuries	12	**AIGREFEUILLE-SUR-MAINE**
	**VIEUX CHÂTEAU	13	*Vendée* **MONTAIGU**
		19	**ST. FULGENT**
	**LES ASPHODELES	20	**CHANTONNAY**
		17	**STE. HERMINE**
71	N.148 *PILORGE	25	**FONTENAY-LE-COMTE** An elegant town on the River Vendée with castle ruins and interesting old houses.
	*Municipal	32	*Deux-Sèvres* **NIORT (Connect Route 14)**
72	N.138	19	**LA CHARRIERE**
		13	*Charente-Maritime* **LOULAY**
	*Du Parc	12	**ST. JEAN D'ANGELY** On the River Boutonne
71	***Municipal	26	**SAINTES** Agreeably situated on the River Charente, an old town with a Triumphal Arch dating back to the Emperor Tiberius. St. Pierre, 12thC; St. Eutrope, 11thC.
	N.137	21	**PONS**
		24	**MIRAMBEAU**
		17	*Gironde* **ETAULIERS**
	D.18	8	**CAVIGNAC**

MICHELIN	ROAD NO.		
MAP NO.	CARAVAN SITES	Km.	

N.10	12	**ST. ANDRÉ-DE-CUBZAC** (Connect Route 13)	
*Municipal *LES GRAVIÈRES	23	**BORDEAUX** (Connect Routes 9, 10, 13, 22, 35)	

Bordeaux, the River Garonne

Route 28 NANTES – POITIERS

MICHELIN MAP NO.	ROAD NO. CARAVAN SITES	Km.	
67	**148 Bis**		*Loire-Atlantique* **NANTES (Connect Routes 11, 27, 29, 45)**
	**Le Moulin	29	**CLISSON**
			Vendée
		27	**MORTAGNE-SUR-SÈVRE** A quaint little town of old walls and gardens above the River Sèvre.
			Deux-Sèvres
	*Le Temple	13	**LE TEMPLE**
		5	**MAULEON**
		22	**BRESSUIRE**
68 67	**La Garenne	31	**PARTHENAY**
			Vienne
		33	**VOUILLE**
68	**MUNICIPAL	15	**POITIERS (Connect Routes 13, 14, 41)**

Route 29 NANTES – ANGERS – LE MANS – CHARTRES – PARIS

MICHELIN MAP NO.	ROAD NO. CARAVAN SITES	Km.	
67	**N.23**		*Loire-Atlantique* **NANTES (Connect Routes 11, 27, 28, 45)**
	*De la Davrays	38	**ANCENIS** Delightfully situated by the suspension bridge over the Loire, this is an interesting old town. Castle ruins, 15thC.
		16	**VARADES**
		21	*Main-et-Loire* **ST. GEORGES-SUR-LOIRE** A small town with a church dating from the 12thC.
64	**PARC DE LA HAYE	18	**ANGERS (Connect Routes 3, 4)**
	*Vallées	24	**SEICHES-SUR-LE-LOIR**
	***International	9	**DURTAL**
		6	*Sarthe* **BAZOUGES-SUR-LE-LOIR**
	**La Route d'Or	7	**LA FLÈCHE** A picturesque town on the Loire. Town Hall in Château des Carmes, 16thC. Military College in Château Neuf, 17thC. St. Thomas, 12thC.
60	*CAMP ST. EXUPÉRY	42	**LE MANS (Connect Routes 2, 34)**
	*LA PLAGE AUX CHAMPS	25	**CONNERRE**
	**La Belle Étoile	21	**LA FERTE-BERNARD** An old fortified town. Notre-Dame, 15thC.
		22	*Eure-et-loir* **NOGENT-LE-ROTROU** The 11thC castle dominates this old town. St. Hilaire, 13thC; Notre-Dame, 12thC.
		37	**COURVILLE-SUR-EURE** There is another castle in this old town, the Château de Villebon.

MICHELIN MAP NO.	ROAD NO. CARAVAN SITES	Km.	
		19	**CHARTRES** (Connect Routes 13, 42)

N.154
N.306
★★★LES QUINCONCES

19 **MAINTENON**

A charming holiday resort. The château dates back to the Middle Ages and was acquired by Louis XIV for Mme de Maintenon.

Seine-et-Oise

★★★★L'ETANG D'OR
★★★Le Pont Hardy

22 **RAMBOUILLET**

Situated in the Forest of Rambouillet, with a château used by the French President as a summer residence. One of the principal meeting-places of hunts in France.

★★★★BOIS-DE-BOULOGNE
(*Closed Jan–Feb only*)
★★★★LE-TREMBLAY
★★★★MAISONS-LAFFITTE
INTERNATIONAL

51 **PARIS**

Summer residence of the French President: Rambouillet

MICHELIN	ROAD NO.		
MAP NO.	CARAVAN SITES	Km.	

86	**N.113**		*Aude*
	***Roche Grise		**NARBONNE (Connect Route 49)**
	**St. Salvayre		Five miles from the Mediterranean up the Canal de la Robine, Narbonne was a seaport in Roman times. It is a most attractive town with a mixture of fine boulevards and narrow streets. St. Just Cath., 14thC with Museum of Religious Art. St. Paul's Basilica, 12thC; Archbishop's Palace, 10thC with Art and History Museum.
	**Municipal	6	**COURSAN**
			Hérault
		11	**NISSAN**
83	*Municipal	10	**BÉZIERS**
			On the River Orb and the Canal du Midi, an old town with a history dating back to Roman times. There is a Garden of Poets and a selection of intriguing buildings. It is said that blancmange was invented here, but the main interest of the town is connected with wine, particularly the red wine known locally as 'Gros rouge'. St.-Nazaire Cath., 12th–14thC; St. Jacques, 12thC. Musée Lapidaire. Musée Fabrégat: pictures, Greek vases. Musée de Vieux Biterroux: Folk museum, also wine.
	*LES CIGALES	22	**PEZENAS**
			An old town, a centre of the wine trade.
		7	**MONTAGNAC**
	**Beau Rivage	12	**MEZE**
		31	**MONTPELLIER (Connect Routes 24, 25)**
		25	**LUNEL**
			An industrial town with a quaint old quarter and pretty gardens.
			Gard
	*MUNICIPAL	26	**NÎMES (Connect Route 32)**
			Capital of Gard, known as the Rome of France, Nimes was an important place in Roman times and there are many reminders of this; a Roman amphitheatre, still

MICHELIN ROAD NO.		
MAP NO.	CARAVAN SITES	Km.

used for bull-fights and other events, a Roman monument, a Roman temple, aqueducts. The principal industries are silk-making and wine. Notre-Dame Cath., 11thC; Clock Tower, 14thC; Museum of Antiquities; Museum of Old Nimes; Natural History Museum.

80	*Les Cyprès	11 **BEZOUCE**

Vaucluse

	****MUNICIPAL	30 **AVIGNON (Connect Routes 6, 16, 36)**
	***BAGATELLE	

The cathedral overlooks the River Orb . . . Béziers

Route 31 NICE – DIGNE – GRENOBLE
(The 'Route Napoleon' – taken on his return from Elba)

MICHELIN MAP NO.	ROAD NO. CARAVAN SITES	Km.	
84	N.202		*Alpes-Maritime* **NICE (Connect Route 6)**
81		63	**PUGET-THÉNIERS** At the junction of the rivers Roudoule and Var, an agreeable old town with a 13thC church.
	N.207 *La Pinède	7	*Basses-Alpes* **ENTREVAUX**
	**Les Iscles	37	**ST.-ANDRÉ-LES-ALPES**
		14	**BARRÈME**
	***MUNICIPAL	30	**DIGNE** On the River Bléone, a pretty place, a popular tourist resort and spa. Napoleon stopped here. St. Jérôme Cath., 15thC; Notre-Dame du Bourg, 12thC.
	N.85 ***Les Salettes	25	**CHÂTEAU-ARNOUX**
		14	**SISTERON** The 14thC cathedral dominates this old town of narrow twisted streets.
	N.75 **Alpes-Provence	18	*Hautes Alpes* **LARAGNE-MONTEGLIN**
		6	**EYGUIANS**
	****DOMAINE DES DEUX SOLEILS ***Des Barillons	11	**SERRES** A charming little village with old houses and an old church.
	*L'Adrech	11	**ASPRES-SUR-BUECH** Junction of the rivers Buech and Chaurune and of roads and railways.
		63	**MONESTIER-DE-CLERMONT**
77	**Les Garcins	18	*Isère* **VIF**

MICHELIN MAP NO.	ROAD NO. CARAVAN SITES	Km.	

| | ***de Varces | 4 | **VARCES** |

17 **GRENOBLE**

Capital of Isère, tourist centre of the French Alps, industrial town and holiday resort, Grenoble is a ski centre with a mountain at the end of each road. The Winter Olympics were held here in 1968. Birthplace of Berlioz and Stendhal. There is an aerial cable railway across the River Isère to a restaurant in what was the Fort de la Bastille. St. André, 13thC; Notre-Dame Cath., 11thC; St. Laurent, 11thC; Stendhal Museum; Natural History Museum; Musée de Peinture: Bonnard, Braque, Chagall, Delacroix, Dufy, Gauguin, Matisse, Monet, Picasso, Renoir, Utrillo.

Ski centre . . . Grenoble (Photo: Cartier-Bresson)

Route 32 NÎMES – VALENCE – ST. ÉTIENNE – ROANNE

MICHELIN MAP NO.	ROAD NO. CARAVAN SITES	Km.	
83	N.86		*Gard*
	*MUNICIPAL		NÎMES (Connect Route 30)
80	***SODOCO	20	PONT-DU-GARD
	**CAMPING-PLAGE		
	**Pont du Gard		
		28	BAGNOLS-SUR-CEZE
	**Municipal	11	PONT-ST.-ESPRIT
			Ardèche
	**Du Lion	15	BOURG ST. ANDEOL
81	**Municipal	15	VIVIERS (Connect Route 16)
80	*Municipal	10	TEIL
		31	VOULTE-SUR-RHÔNE
77	***LES VOILIERS	3	BEAUCHASTEL
		18	ST. PERAY
76	***Municipal	15	TOURNON
	**Les Sables		On the Rhône, a fascinating old town with a 16thC lycée, the oldest in the country, also a 16thC castle.
	N.82		
	**L'Iserand	6	VION
			Loire
		39	BOURG-ARGENTAL
73	**CHANTEGRILLET	29	ST. ÉTIENNE
			On the River Furan, capital of Loire, an industrial town in a coal-mining area, but also a tourist centre. St. Étienne, 14thC; Museum: Pictures, weapons. Industrial Museum.
		41	FEURS (Connect Route 22)
		9	BALBIGNY
	*MUNICIPAL	31	ROANNE (Connect Route 41)
			On the Loire, an industrial town and port. St. Étienne, 13thC.

Route 33 ORLÉANS — SENS — TROYES — NANCY

MICHELIN MAP NO.	ROAD NO. CARAVAN SITES	Km.	
64	N.152 **Municipal		*Loiret* **ORLÉANS (Connect Routes 34, 37, 42, 48)** On the River Loire and capital of Loiret, the town will always be associated with Joan of Arc who defeated the English here in 1429 (celebrated on 8 May annually). In its time it has been attacked by Julius Caesar, Attila, Clovis, the Prussians, the Italians and the Germans, but it is now an elegant town of boulevards and gardens and fascinating old houses. Floral park, one of the most magnificent flower shows in Europe, April– October. St. Euvarte, 12thC; Cath. from 13thC, with windows depicting Joan of Arc. Musée des Beaux Arts: Boucher, Fragonard, Ingres, Poussin, Watteau.
		25	**CHÂTEAUNEUF-SUR-LOIRE**
	N.60	23	**BELLEGARDE**
61	**Le Huillard	14	**ST. MAURICE-SUR-FESSARD**
65 61	***MUNICIPAL	9	**MONTARGIS (Connect Route 38)** On the Canal du Loing, the Canal d'Orléans and the Canal de Briare, a picturesque old town and good fishing area. Madeleine, 12thC.

Statue of Joan of Arc . . . Orléans

		Km.	
		26	**COURTENAY**

Yonne

27 **SENS**
On the River Yonne, a town of importance in Celtic and in Roman times. Until the mid-17thC the bishops of Paris took their orders from the archbishop of Sens. The Cathedral (1140), is one of the first French Gothic buildings; in the Treasury may be seen a large ivory chest and liturgical comb of St. Lupus, 7thC, ancient fabrics, Byzantine shrouds, the chasuble of Thomas à Becket, tapestries etc.

N.5
N.60   22 **VILLENEUVE-L'ARCHEVEQUE**

Aube

***Municipal   42 **TROYES (Connect Route 7)**

21 **PINEY**

19 **BRIENNE-LE-CHÂTEAU**
Napoleon studied here for five years from 1779 at the École Militaire and here, also, he won a victory over Blücher in 1814. The château was built for the Brienne family. Musée Napoleon.

Haute-Marne
31 **DOULEVANT-LE-CHÂTEAU**

66   **Le Petit Bois   22 **JOINVILLE (Connect Route 21)**

Meuse
49 **VAUCOULEURS**
An old walled town. Here, in 1429, Joan of Arc asked the governor, Robert de Baudricourt, to provide an escort to take her to Charles VII. The nearby village of Domrémy is the birthplace of Joan and her house may still be seen.

Meurthe-et-Moselle
62   ***Municipal   24 **TOUL (Connect Route 39)**
An old fortified town. St. Étienne Cath., 13thC; St. Gengoult, 13thC.

N.4
***DE BRABOIS   23 **NANCY (Connect Routes 5, 26, 39)**

Route 34 ORLÉANS – LE MANS – RENNES – ST. BRIEUC – BREST

MICHELIN MAP NO.	ROAD NO. CARAVAN SITES	Km.	
64	**N.826** ****Municipal**		*Loiret* **ORLÉANS (Connect Routes 33, 37, 42, 48)**
		31	*Loir-et-Cher* **OUZOUER-LE-MARCHE**
		62	*Sarthe* **ST. CALAIS** An old town with an interesting museum, art gallery and a Benedictine monastery.
		16	**BOULOIRE**
60	***CAMP ST. EXUPÉRY**	29	**LE MANS (Connect Routes 2, 29)**
	N.157	38	**ST. DENIS-D'ORQUES**
	**La Rousine	33	*Mayenne* **LAVAL** An industrial town on the River Mayenne with two old castles. St. Martin, 11thC; Cathedral, 11thC.
		35	**Ile-et-Vilaine** **VITRE** On the River Vilaine, a charming old town with narrow streets, overlooked by its 11thC castle with a drawbridge and impressive towers. Notre-Dame, 15thC.
		15	**CHÂTEAUBOURG**
59		21	**RENNES (Connect Routes 1, 45)**
	N.12	31	**MONTAUBAN**
		21	*Côtes-du-Nord* **BROONS**
58		27	**LAMBALLE** On the River Gouessan, a pleasant town noted for its stud farm. Notre-Dame, 12thC.

***MUNICIPAL**   23   **ST. BRIEUC**
Capital of Côtes-du-Nord and an agreeable tourist centre. St. Étienne Cath., 13thC. Museum: Jordaens, Tintoretto.

18   **CHATELAUDREN**

14   **GUINGAMP**
A town with ramparts, narrow streets, and the remains of an old castle.

19   **BELLE-ISLE-EN-TERRE**

Finistère

Langolvas   35   **MORLAIX**
An old town with a harbour although it is some miles inland; there is also an enormous viaduct. Château de Taureau, 16thC.

39   **LANDERNEAU**
A market town with charming old houses. Although some miles from the sea it is a port, also a centre of salmon fishing.

Ste. Anne-du-Portzic   21   BREST (Connect Route 11)
ST. MARC

Rennes

Route 35 PAU – BORDEAUX

MICHELIN MAP NO.	ROAD NO. CARAVAN SITES	Km.	

85	**N.134** **DU COY **LES SAPINS		*Basses-Pyrénées* **PAU (Connect Route 8)**
82	***Les Ombrages de l'Adour	44	**AIRE-SUR-L'ADOUR** *Landes*
		21	**VILLENEUVE-DE-MARSAN**
		17	**ROQUEFORT**
	N.132	28	*Gironde* **CAPTIEUX**
79	*La Forêt	9	**BEAULAC**
		7	**BAZAS** The interest of this small town centres around its cathedral which has been destroyed and rebuilt several times. The town is situated quite dramatically with ancient ramparts upon a rocky perch.
	**Allées Marine	16	**LANGON (Connect Route 10)**
71	**N.113**	14	**PODENSAC (Connect Route 10)**
	*Municipal *LES GRAVIÈRES	32	**BORDEAUX (Connect Routes 9, 10, 13, 22, 27)**

Route 36 PARIS – AUXERRE – CHALON-SUR-SAÔNE – MÂCON – LYON – VALENCE – AVIGNON

MICHELIN	ROAD NO.	
MAP NO.	CARAVAN SITES	Km.

The Autoroute du Sud, the fastest and easiest route to and from the Mediterranean; 700 km. of road upon which it is possible to maintain the maximum permitted speed for hour after hour, with stops only necessary for the payment of tolls. Petrol stations, café/restaurants, parking lay-bys with toilets are spaced at regular intervals.

Camping Sites adjacent to the A.6/7 are shown since night stops are advisable. It will be appreciated that the appropriate Junction at which to come off the Autoroute must be ascertained in advance from map and Toll Card. Although all exits will obviously be to the RIGHT, to assist in map reading the letter (R) or (L) against each place-name indicates whether the site lies to the RIGHT or LEFT of the Autoroute.

61	****BOIS-DE-BOULOGNE		**PARIS**
	(*Closed Jan–Feb only*)		
	****LE-TREMBLAY		
	****MAISONS-LAFFITTE		
	INTERNATIONAL		

A.6 — *Seine-et-Marne*

***Camp de l'A.C.C.C.F.   82   (R) **NEMOURS (Connect Route 38)**
A handsome old fortified town in the Loing valley with a 12thC castle, now a museum containing Gallo-Roman exhibits, Antwerp tapestries, pictures.

Yonne

65   ***MUNICIPAL   83   (R) **AUXERRE**
Splendidly situated on the River Yonne, a charming little town with narrow streets and a centre of wine-growing and cherry orchards. St. Étienne Cath., 13thC; St. Pierre, 16thC; St. Germain crypt, 858; Clock Tower, 15thC.

*Vieux Moulin   (R) **CRAVANT**

***Sous-Roche   (R) **AVALLON**
A pretty little town. Clock Tower, 15thC, and ramparts. St. Lazare, 11thC.

Côte d'Or

(L) **SEMUR-EN-AUXOIS**
On the River Armançon, a delightful small town with an 11thC church, Notre-Dame.

DE L'HÔTEL DE VILLE   (R) **PRÉCY-SOUS-THIL

MICHELIN MAP NO.	ROAD NO. CARAVAN SITES	Km.	
69	***Les Cent Vignes		(R) **BEAUNE (Connect Route 12)**
	***La Grappe d'Or		(R) **MEURSAULT (Connect Route 12)**
	***Pâquier-Fané		*Saône-et-Loire* (R) **CHAGNY (Connect Route 12)**
	****MUNICIPAL	175	(L) **CHALON-SUR-SAÔNE (Connect Route 12)**
	**Le Pas Fleury		(L) **TOURNUS (Connect Route 12)**
	****Le National 6		(R) **UCHIZY**
70	**ST. PIERRE		(R) **LUGNY**
69	**Des Grottes		(R) **AZE**
	***Des Peupliers		*Ain* (L) **PONT-DE-VAUX**
70 69	****MUNICIPAL	60	*Saône-et-Loire* (L) **MÂCON (Connect Route 4)**
73 74	**Municipal		(R) **CRECHES-SUR-SAÔNE**
73	**Beaujolais		(L) **ST. ROMAIN-DES-ILES**
	****Camping-Plage		*Ain* (L) **THOISSEY**
74	****Municipal Sud		(L) **MONTMERLE-SUR-SAÔNE**
73	**De Ludna		*Rhône* (R) **ST. GEORGES-DE-RENEINS**
	**Bords de Saône		*Ain* (L) **BEAUREGARD**
74	**Municipal		*Rhône* (R) **VILLEFRANCHE-SUR-SAÔNE** An industrial town, a centre for Beaujolais wine. Notre-Dame, 12thC.
	****Idéal Camping		*Ain* (L) **JASSANS-RIOTTIER**
	***La Petite Saône		(L) **TREVOUX**

The Forum, Vienne

MICHELIN MAP NO.	ROAD NO. CARAVAN SITES	Km.	
			Rhône
73	**International Camping		(R) **ANSE**
74	**A.7**		
73	****PORTE DU LYON	70	**LYON (Connect Routes 22, 26, 41)**
			Isère
	**Leveau		(R) **VIENNE**
			A town of importance in Roman times, now a centre of industry on the banks of the Rhône. St. Pierre, 10thC; St. Maurice Cath., 12thC. Roman temple and other remains.
			Ardèche
76	****Château de Peyraud		(R) **PEYRAUD**
			Drôme
77	**Les Claires		(R) **ST. RAMBERT D'ALBON**
	****Château de Sénaud		(L) **ALBON**
76	**LES LUCS		(R) **TAIN L'HERMITAGE**
77		100	**VALENCE (Connect Route 50)**
76			On the River Rhône, capital of Drôme, a busy town that dates back to Roman times. Somewhat damaged in WW2. St. Apollinaire Cath., 11thC.
77	*Scipion-L'Africain		(L) **LIVRON-SUR-DRÔME**
80	***LES DEUX SAISONS		(R) **MONTÉLIMAR**
81			Chiefly famous for the manufacture of nougat; shops and stalls line the roads into the town, all selling nougat. Remains of 11thC château.
			Vaucluse
	***Beauregard		(L) **MORNAS**
	**St. Eutrope		(L) **ORANGE (Connect Route 16)**
	****MUNICIPAL	125	**AVIGNON (Connect Routes 6, 16, 30)**
	***BAGATELLE		

MICHELIN MAP NO.	ROAD NO. CARAVAN SITES	Km.	
64	****BOIS-DE-BOULOGNE (*Closed Jan–Feb only*) ****LE-TREMBLAY ****MAISONS-LAFFITTE INTERNATIONAL		**PARIS**
	N.20		*Essonne*
		35	**ARPAJON** A small town of Gallo-Roman origin with a picturesque market place. It is an agricultural centre.
			Seine-et-Oise
		19	**ETAMPES** A royal town until the 14thC. Imposingly situated, with a vast tower and remains of the 12thC royal castle. St. Basile, 12thC; St. Martin, 12thC; Notre-Dame, 12thC. Museum: Gallo-Roman, 18thC pictures.
		18	**ANGERVILLE**
			Eure-et-Loir
		14	**TOURY**
			Loiret
		14	**ARTENAY (Connect Route 42)**
	**Municipal	20	**ORLÉANS (Connect Routes 33, 34, 42, 48)**
	N.152 *Municipal	18	**MEUNG-SUR-LOIRE**
	***Val de Flux	7	**BEAUGENCY** On the River Loire. Joan of Arc won a victory over the English here in 1429. Old castle and abbey.
			Loire-et-Cher
	****La Grenouillère	5	**SUÈVRES**
		8	**MER**
	***LA BOIRE	19	**BLOIS** On the River Loire with the famous royal castle above, containing five centuries of history and memories of Louis XII, Francis I, Gaston d'Orleans and Catherine

de Medici. Here the fate of the Kingdom of France
was decided between Henri III and the Duc de Guise.
Blois is a most beautiful place and a convenient centre
from which to visit all the other castles of the Loire.
Capital of the département, Blois is noted for the
manufacture of chocolate. St. Nicholas, 12thC; St.
Louis Cath., 11thC.

Indre-et-Loire

***L'Isle d'Or   45   **AMBOISE**
An old town on the Loire noted for its royal palace.
Leonardo da Vinci died here in 1519.

16   **VOUVRAY**

L'ALOUETTE   10   **TOURS (Connect Routes 2, 4, 13)

Five centuries of history . . . Blois

225

Route 38 PARIS – NEVERS – MOULINS – VICHY – CLERMONT-FERRAND

MICHELIN MAP NO.	ROAD NO. CARAVAN SITES	Km.	
61	****BOIS-DE-BOULOGNE (*Closed Jan–Feb only*) ****LE-TREMBLAY ****MAISONS-LAFFITTE INTERNATIONAL		**PARIS**
	N.7		*Seine-et-Marne*
		52	**FONTAINEBLEAU** A royal town famous for its palace and the forest surrounding it; with the richest share of history of any castle in France, from Louis VII to Napoleon III. Military Museum: uniforms.
	***Camp de l'A.C.C.C.F.	32	**NEMOURS (Connect Route 36)**
		11	**SOUPPES**
	**Municipal	5	*Loiret* **DORDIVES**
	*Nargis-Fontenay	5	**FONTENAY-SUR-LOING**
	***MUNICIPAL	13	**MONTARGIS (Connect Route 33)**
		22	**LES BEZARDS**
65	**Le Martinet	19	**BRIARE** Eiffel's bridge, 640 m. long, built in 1890 to carry the Briare Canal over the River Loire, is the principal item of interest.
	*Du Val	12	**BONNY-S-LOIRE**
	***L'ILE DE COSNE	19	*Nièvre* **COSNE-S-LOIRE** An industrial centre whose ironworks once catered for the shipping industry in the making of anchors, cannon, etc. St. Agnan, 12thC. Musée de la Loire.
		15	**POUILLY**
	**La Saulaie	13	**LA CHARITÉ-S-LOIRE** An old town, once a busy port. It was also a place of pilgrimage, hence its name. Ste. Croix, 11thC.

MICHELIN MAP NO.	ROAD NO. / CARAVAN SITES	Km.	
		14	**POUGES**
69	**★★MUNICIPAL**	11	**NEVERS (Connect Route 4)**
		24	**ST. PIERRE-LE-MONTIER**
			Allier
	★★Camping-Plage	32	**MOULINS (Connect Route 5)**
	★★★de Chazeuil	30	**VARENNES-S-ALLIER (Connect Route 41)**
	N.493	14	**ST. GERMAIN-DES-FOSSES**
		9	**CUSSET** An ancient town at the foot of Montagne Bourbonnaise.
73	**★★★★Les Acacias-Plage** **★★★★Beau-Rivage** **★★★★Nouvelle Europe** **★★MUNICIPAL**	4	**VICHY** Principally famous for its spa and Vichy Water, which was known in Roman times, but whose prosperity dates from the time of Henry IV. Napoleon created the Parc de Sources in 1810. Marshal Pétain's government set up in Vichy from 1940 to 1944. Although dominated by the spa treatment centres it is a popular holiday resort with English-type gardens of flowers, casino, beautiful shops.
			Puy-de-Dôme
		14	**RANDAN** A pleasant town on the edge of a beautiful forest of oak trees.
		13	**MARINGUES**
		16	**PONT-DU-CHÂTEAU** There is good salmon fishing here.
	N.89	15	**CLERMONT-FERRAND (Connect Routes 16, 22, 25)**
61	**★★★★BOIS-DE-BOULOGNE** *(Closed Jan–Feb only)* **★★★★LE-TREMBLAY** **★★★★MAISONS-LAFFITTE** INTERNATIONAL		**PARIS**

Route 39 PARIS − NANCY − STRASBOURG

MICHELIN MAP NO.	ROAD NO. CARAVAN SITES	Km.	
			Meurthe-et-Moselle
	★★★Municipal	23	**TOUL (Connect Route 33)**
	★★★DE BRABOIS	23	**NANCY (Connect Routes 5, 26, 33)**
		12	**ST. NICOLAS-DE-PORT**
		4	**DOMBASLE**
		14	**LUNEVILLE** A gracious town with the 18thC castle of the Dukes of Lorraine, now a museum.
		30	**BLAMONT** There are splendid grottoes here, also the old castle of the Count of Montbeliard.
			Moselle
		24	**SARREBOURG** On the River Sarre. 13thC church and small museum.
	★★LE VIEUX CHÂTEAU	16	**PHALSBOURG**
			Bas-Rhin
	★★BELVEDERE	26	**SAVERNE** A rose-growing centre with a beautiful 18thC rose-coloured castle in a park on the banks of the Canal de la Marne au Rhin.
87	★★★★La Montagne Vert ★★★DU BAGGERSEE	41	**STRASBOURG** Capital of Bas-Rhin and of Alsace, situated on the Rhine, a big commercial port with a history going back to Roman times. It was in the German Empire until taken by Louis XIV; in 1870 it became German again after the Franco-German War; after WW1 it reverted to France. There is a statue to Gutenberg whose printing press was perfected in Strasbourg. The Council of Europe sits here, together with the European Court for the Rights of Man. St. Thomas, 13thC; rose-coloured Gothic cathedral in Vosges sandstone, 420 ft. spire, astronomical clock. Château des Rohans, now a museum; Musée des Beaux Arts: Bonnard, Boucher, Braque, Corot, Degas, Dufy, El Greco, Fragonard, Gauguin, Monet, Pissarro, Rembrandt, Renoir, Rubens, Sisley, Van Dyck, Watteau. Arts Décoratifs Museum: Enamels, ironwork, clocks. There are tours

of Strasbourg by boat, a thrilling experience at night through the floodlit city. At nearby Kintzheim, on the 'Wine Road', is the Volerie des Aigles, a unique falconry with a great variety of birds of prey.

Strasbourg

Route 40 PARIS — CHÂLONS-SUR-MARNE — VERDUN — METZ

MICHELIN MAP NO.	ROAD NO. CARAVAN SITES	Km.	
56	****BOIS-DE-BOULOGNE (*Closed Jan–Feb only*) ****LE-TREMBLAY ****MAISONS-LAFFITTE INTERNATIONAL		**PARIS**
	N.3	23	**VILLEPARISIS**
	**DE LA PLAGE DE TRILPORT	21	*Seine-et-Marne* **MEAUX** On the River Marne, an old town of Gallic origin. St. Étienne Cath., 12thC.
	N.33	19	**LA FERTE**
		34	*Marne* **MONTMIRAIL** Here, in 1814, Napoleon won a victory over the Prussians. Castle remains and ramparts.
	N.3 ****Municipal	64	**CHÂLONS-SUR-MARNE (Connect Route 21)**
		43	**STE. MENEHOULD** Dom Pérignon, who invented the formula for champagne, was born here.
		15	**CLERMONT-EN-ARGONNE**
		27	*Meuse* **VERDUN-SUR-MEUSE** With a history going back to Roman times, Verdun is probably best known for its association with WWI; it is, in fact, a centre for the tour of the battlefields. There are over twenty cemeteries, one French, with fifteen thousand graves. Verdun is now a lively commercial town with a 12thC cathedral that has survived the destruction of war.
57		64	*Moselle* **METZ** Capital of Moselle, on the rivers Moselle and Seille, a large industrial town that dates back to Roman times. There are old houses and streets but the accent is on industry. St. Étienne Cath., 13thC; St. Martin, 12thC.

Route 41 POITIERS – MONTLUÇON – ROANNE – LYON

MICHELIN MAP NO.	ROAD NO. CARAVAN SITES	Km.	
67	**N.151** **MUNICIPAL		*Vienne* **POITIERS (Connect Routes 13, 14, 28)**
68	***LA FONTAINE	23	**CHAUVIGNY**
		19	**ST. SAVIN**
		18	*Indre* **LE BLANC**
		22	**ST. GAULTIER (Connect Route 14)**
	N.727 **Les Chambons	10	**ARGENTON-SUR-CREUSE (Connect Route 48)** A charming little place with quaint old houses. St. Benedict, 15thC.
		23	**NEUVY-ST.-SEPULCHRE**
		16	**LA CHÂTRE** An old town with a museum in the castle devoted to the works and memories of George Sand who spent much of her life here.
	N.143	34	*Cher* **CHÂTEAUMEILLANT**
		13	**CULAN** On the River Arnon. 15thC castle.
69	**LE MAS *Municipal	33	*Allier* **MONTLUÇON (Connect Route 5)**
	N.145 **Le Boutillon	9	**CHAMBLET (Connect Route 5)**
		22	**MONTMARAULT (Connect Route 5)**
	N.146 *Municipal	30	**ST. POURCAIN-SUR-SIOULE** Surrounded by famous vineyards this little town contains the church of Ste. Croix, a former Benedictine abbey dating back to the 10thC.

| | **N.7**
***de Chazeuil | 10 | **VARENNES-SUR-ALLIER (Connect Route 38)** |

21 **LAPALISSE**
On the River Besbre, with a huge 15thC château in which are magnificent French tapestries. In twenty miles on the N.480, along the Besbre valley, are the châteaux . . . de Gléné, 18thC . . . de Trézelles, 15thC . . . de Chavroches (ruins) . . . du Grand-Chambord . . . de Jaligny . . . de Beauvoir and de Thoury.

Loire

73   *MUNICIPAL   48 **ROANNE (Connect Route 32)**

44 **TARARE**
In a wooded setting, a small town of mills with a 16thC tower.

Rhône

73
74   ****PORTE DE LYON   44 **LYON (Connect Routes 22, 26, 36)**

Route 42 ROUEN – EVREUX – CHARTRES – ORLÉANS

MICHELIN MAP NO.	ROAD NO. CARAVAN SITES	Km.	
55	**N.13 BIS** **ROUEN-BONSECOURS		*Seine-Maritime* **ROUEN (Connect Routes 1, 19, 43, 44)**
	**Eure-et-Seine	17	*Eure* **PONT-DE-L'ARCHE**
		11	**LOUVIERS**
	**Municipal	24	**EVREUX (Connect Route 15)**
	N.154	29	**NONANCOURT** An old town with a history that recalls Henry I and Richard Lionheart.
60	**N.12** **Pre de l'Eglise	3	*Eure-et-Loire* **ST. RÉMY-S-AVRE**
		10	**DREUX** A town set in charming countryside, steeped in history from Roman times. In the small museum are two Louise Quinze consoles from the Crécy Château of the Marquise de Pompadour. St. Pierre, 13thC.
	N.154	36	**CHARTRES (Connect Routes 13, 29)**
		52	*Loiret* **ARTENAY (Connect Route 37)**
64	**N.20** **Municipal	20	**ORLÉANS (Connect Routes 33, 34, 37, 48)**

Route 43 ROUEN – PARIS
(there is an alternative route by Autoroute A.13)

MICHELIN MAP NO.	ROAD NO. CARAVAN SITES	Km.	
55	**N.14** ****ROUEN-BONSECOURS		*Seine-Maritime* **ROUEN (Connect Routes, 1, 19, 42, 44)**
	**LES POMMIERS	10	**BOOS**
		12	**FLEURY-S-ANDELLE**
		42	*Val-d'Oise* **MAGNY-EN-VEXIN** An ancient town once encircled by ramparts.
		27	*Seine-et-Oise* **PONTOISE** An old stronghold with narrow streets. Pissarro lived here. St. Maclou, 12thC; Notre-Dame, 16thC.
	****BOIS-DE-BOULOGNE (*Closed Jan–Feb only*) ****LE-TREMBLAY ****MAISONS-LAFFITTE INTERNATIONAL	30	**PARIS**

Route 44 ROUEN – BEAUVAIS – SOISSONS – REIMS (RHEIMS)

MICHELIN MAP NO.	ROAD NO. CARAVAN SITES	Km.	
55	**N.30** **ROUEN-BONSECOURS		*Seine-Maritime* **ROUEN (Connect Routes 1, 19, 42, 43)**
		51	**GOURNAY-EN-BRAY** It is said that cream cheese was invented here and the manufacture of this is now the principal industry of this small town.
	N.31 **MUNICIPAL	30	*Oise* **BEAUVAIS (Connect Route 17)**
		12	**BRESLES**
		13	**CLERMONT** An old town with a 13thC Town Hall and a 12thC keep. St. Samson, 13thC.

A most popular tourist attraction . . . Compiègne

56	***L'Hippodrome	31	**COMPIÈGNE**

A popular place for tourists with the attractions of the great palace and the enormous forest (33,000 acres and one of the largest in France), a favourite hunting-ground of the kings of France. Joan of Arc was captured here on 23 May 1430 by John of Luxembourg, who handed her over to the English. The palace is now a museum. The rooms occupied by Marie Antoinette, Napoleon I and III can be seen. There is also the National Automobile Museum with 150 vehicles ranging from the Roman chariot to the Citroën chain-track car. Nearby in the forest is the clearing in which Marshal Foch received the German surrender in November 1918 – and in which Hitler received the French surrender in 1940. The original railway saloon car was destroyed in WW2 but a replica is on view. In the Town Hall Museum is a museum of historical miniature figures, the only French museum of lead soldiers (90,000), with a large depiction of the Battle of Waterloo.

Aisne

	**Municipal	39	**SOISSONS (Connect Route 23)**
		18	**BRAINE**

A small town with a Premonstratensian abbey church, 12thC.

Marne

		12	**FISMES**
	***Camp de Champagne	28	**REIMS (Connect Route 21)**

Route 45 ST. MALO – RENNES – NANTES

MICHELIN	ROAD NO.	
MAP NO.	CARAVAN SITES	**Km.**

The beach, St. Malo

59	**N.137** **La Grand Grève		*Île-et-Vilaine* **ST. MALO** An enchanting and historic seaport; with its town walls it still resembles a medieval fortress. The name of the town is derived from a Welsh monk. Much damaged in WW2 and rebuilt on original lines. St. Vincent, 13thC; Castle, 14thC.
		14	**CHATEAUNEUF**
		14	**ST. PIERRE-DE-PLESQUEN**
	**Ille et Rance	8	**ST. DOMINUEC**
	**LE LOGIS *MUNICIPAL	6	**TINTENIAC**
		5	**HEDE**
		22	**RENNES (Connect Routes 1, 34)**
		32	**BAIN-DE-BRETAGNE**
		22	*Loire-Atlantique* **DERVAL**
		13	**NOZAY**
67		41	**NANTES (Connect Routes 11, 27, 28, 29)**

Route 46 TARBES – TOULOUSE – ALBI – ST. FLOUR

MICHELIN MAP NO.	ROAD NO. CARAVAN SITES	Km.	
85	**N.21** **LES HORIZONS		*Hautes-Pyrénées* **TARBES (Connect Route 8)**
82		20	**RABASTENS**
	***LE LAC **BERROY-CAMPING	16	*Gers* **MIELAN**
	*LE BATARDEAU	14	**MIRANDE**
	*L'ILE ST. MARTIN	25	**AUCH** On the River Gers, an attractive old town, capital of Gers and once capital of Gascony. The main item of interest is the striking 15thC cathedral.
	N.124	16	**GIMONT** Ancient fortified town dating from 1265, with an old covered market.
		19	**L'ISLE-JOURDAIN** A pretty little town with a delightful market.
		15	*Haute-Garonne* **LEGUEVIN**
	***MUNICIPAL	17	**TOULOUSE (Connect Routes 10, 47, 48, 49)**

The city of Toulouse

MAP NO.	CARAVAN SITES	Km.	
	N.88	20	**MONASTRUC-LA-CONSEILLERE**
			Tarn
		17	**RABASTENS**
		8	**LISLE**
	**Le Lido	9	**GAILLAC**

Quaint old town with arcade and the fountain of Griffoul. St. Pierre, 12thC; Museum: Fine arts, history of Gaillac wine.

	**Plage du Lac	11	**RIVIÈRE**
	***DE CAUSSELS	11	**ALBI**

On the River Tarn and capital of Tarn, an old town of fine medieval, red-brick buildings, particularly the 13thC cathedral of Ste.-Cécile towering massively over the town. Toulouse-Lautrec Museum in the 13thC La Berbie Palace. Toulouse-Lautrec was born at Albi (1864), and there is here the most important collection in the world of his works; also Degas, Bonnard, Matisse, Utrillo, Dufy. St. Salvi, 12thC.

79	****De la Verrerie**	16	**CARMAUX**
			Avreyon
		56	**LA PRIMAUBE**
		9	**RODEZ**

An old town built around the 13thC Gothic cathedral. There is a pleasant market here.

		21	**ROTONDE**
	**Roc de l'Arche	11	**ESPALION**

On the River Lot with the ruins of a 12thC castle.

76	**N.121** ***La Roseaie**	24	**LAGUIOLE**
			Cantal
	**Le Tillet	18	**JABRUN**
	**Le Couffour	13	**CHAUDES-AIGUES**

A well-known spa in the Remontalou valley; its waters were known to the Romans. It is the only locality in Europe heated by the canalization of natural hot water.

	***Les Orgues ****Du Lander**	30	**ST. FLOUR (Connect Route 25)**

Route 47 TOULOUSE − FOIX − BOURG-MADAME

MICHELIN MAP NO.	ROAD NO. CARAVAN SITES	Km.	
82	**N.20** ***MUNICIPAL		*Haut-Garonne* **TOULOUSE (Connect Routes 10, 46, 48, 49)**
		23	**VERNET**
		11	**AUTERIVE**
		15	*Ariège* **SAVERDUN**
	***MUNICIPAL	16	**PAMIERS** A town of pleasant boulevards and the ruins of an abbey. St. Antonin Cath., 17thC.
	**Parc du Château	9	**VARILHES**
86	**Lac de Labarre	10	**FOIX (Connect Route 8)**
	**PRE LOMBARD	16	**TARASCON** A town of heavy industry.
		3	**USSAT**
		8	**LES CABANNES**
	***MALAZEOU	16	**AX-LES-THERMES** A town of many hot sulphur springs that were popular in Roman times. It is also a holiday and mountaineering centre.

From here the road is difficult for caravans.

	***Le Robinson	50	*Pyrénées-Orientales* **ENVEITG**
	***DU SEGRE **L'Aiglon	6	**BOURG-MADAME** A small village on the Spanish border.

Route 48 TOULOUSE – CAHORS – BRIVE – LIMOGES – CHÂTEAUROUX – VIERZON – ORLÉANS

MICHELIN MAP NO.	ROAD NO. CARAVAN SITES	Km.	
82	**N.20** ***MUNICIPAL		*Haut-Garonne* **TOULOUSE (Connect Routes 10, 46, 47, 49)**
	**Aquitaine-Camping	29	*Tarn-et-Garonne* **GRISOLLES (Connect Route 10)**
79	***ALSACE	23	**MONTAUBAN** Capital of Tarn-et-Garonne and situated above the River Tarn, this is a most handsome town. The 17thC bishop's palace, once a castle, looks out over the 14thC brick-built Pont du Tarn with seven arches. St. Jacques, 14thC. Musée Ingres: 4,000 drawings by Ingres, who was a native of the town.
	***Château St. Marcel	16	**REALVILLE**
	**LA PIBOULETTE	7	**CAUSSADE** An old town with a number of 13thC buildings.
	**La Chaumière *ST. GEORGES	40	*Lot* **CAHORS** Situated on, and almost surrounded by, the divisions of the River Lot and capital of the département of Lot, Cahors is an old town, a capital in Roman times. The stone-built bridge, over 600 years old, has been called the most beautiful bridge in the world. Many streets in France are named 'Gambetta'; Léon Gambetta, born in Cahors in 1838, was a political leader who achieved his fame by standing up to the Prussians in 1870. Cahors is a most picturesque town with parts of ramparts and guard-gates remaining, also a Roman archway. Palace of Pope John XXII; St. Étienne Cath., 12thC. Château du Roi, 14thC; Museum: lapidary, coins and medals.
	**TIRELIRE	33	**FRAYSSINET**
75	****Les Pins	35	**PAYRAC**
	****LA DRAILLE **Les Ondines	14	**SOUILLAC** On the rivers Borrèze and Dordogne, best known for its fine 12thC Romanesque church with interesting sculptures.

242

MICHELIN MAP NO.	ROAD NO. CARAVAN SITES	Km.	
			Corrèze
74	★★★LA FERME DES ILES	36	**BRIVE-LA-GAILLARDE (Connect Route 22)**
	★★Bourgeolle	11	**DONZENAC**
		14	**PERPEZAC-LE-NOIR**
75		12	**UZERCHE**
			An old town above the River Vézère with a unique clock tower in the 14thC church.
			Haut-Vienne
72	★★★Les Ecureuils	27	**MAGNAC-BOURG**
		12	**PIERRE-BUFFIÈRE**
	★★★★MUNICIPAL	20	**LIMOGES**
			On the River Vienne, capital of Haut-Vienne with a history dating back before Roman times. Limoges china is, of course, famous throughout the world.

Visit Limoges to see the Museum of Porcelain, the largest in the world

Enamels have been produced here since the 5thC and there is a collection in the Municipal Museum, once the Bishop's Palace. Also in the National Museum is a fine collection of ceramics from all over the world in addition to the French porcelain exhibited. There are two old bridges over the River Vienne, St. Martial, 12thC and St. Étienne, 13thC. St. Étienne Cath., 13thC; St. Pierre, 13thC.

	**Les Roussilles	18	**LA CROUZILLE**
		16	**BESSINES**
		12	**LA CROISIÈRE**

Indre

68	**RELAIS	37	**CELON**
	**Les Chambons	9	**ARGENTON-S-CREUSE (Connect Route 41)**
	***LE ROCHAT	30	**CHÂTEAUROUX (Connect Route 14)**
	**Les Pins		
		30	**VATAN**

St. Laurian church, 15thC, is of interest, also the Maison de la Perrine, 12thC.

Cher

	**Bellon-Plage	27	**VIERZON (Connect Route 4)**

Loir-et-Cher

		23	**SALBRIS**
	***La Grande Sologne	13	**NOUAN-LE-FUZELIER**
		6	**LAMOTTE-BEUVRON**

Loiret

	*Municipal	15	**LA FERTE-ST. AUBIN**
	**Pont Bouchet	18	**OLIVET**
	**Municipal	5	**ORLÉANS (Connect Routes 33, 34, 37, 42)**

Route 49 TOULOUSE — CARCASSONNE — NARBONNE

MICHELIN MAP NO.	ROAD NO. CARAVAN SITES	Km.	
82	**N.113** ***MUNICIPAL		*Haut-Garonne* **TOULOUSE (Connect Routes 10, 46, 47, 48)**
		11	**CASTANET**
		8	**MONTGISCARD**
		15	**VILLEFRANCHE-DE-LAURAGAIS** A small market town with a 14thC Gothic church built of brick.
	**Municipal	23	*Aude* **CASTELNAUDARY** A particular form of stew called cassoulet originated here. It is a small town with a 14thC church, St. Michel.
	*Municipal	12	**VILLEPINTE**

Unique example of a fortified town . . . Carcassonne

MICHELIN MAP NO.	ROAD NO. CARAVAN SITES	Km.	
		8	**ALZONNE**
83	***Les Lavandières **ALBERT DOMEC	17	**CARCASSONNE**

Capital of Aude on the River Aude, a very old town of particular interest because it still retains its medieval walls, fifty-four towers and the battlements of fifteen centuries; the whole of the new town is not now contained within them. The Cité is a unique example of a fortified medieval town, probably the finest in Europe and absolutely complete, having been much restored. St. Nazaire, 11thC; 12thC Castle and Museum.

		19	**CAPENDU**
86	***LA PINÈDE	18	**LÉZIGNAN-CORBIÈRES**
	***Roche Gris **St. Salvayre	20	**NARBONNE** (Connect Route 30)

Route 50 VALENCE — CHAMBÉRY — AIX-LES-BAINS — ANNECY — GENEVA (Switzerland)

MICHELIN MAP NO.	ROAD NO. CARAVAN SITES	Km.	
77	**N.92**		*Drôme* **VALENCE (Connect Route 36)**
	**Parc des Sports	17	**BOURG-DE-PÉAGE**
	*L'Aéro-Club	1	**ROMANS-SUR-ISÈRE** An old town attractively situated across the River Isère from Bourg-de-Péage (so called because there used to be a toll for crossing the bridge). Romans-sur-Isère is mainly a manufacturing town specializing in footwear, but there are the remains of an old wall and an abbey.
		26	*Isère* **ST. MARCELLIN** An ancient town with 13thC town walls and castle ruins of the same era.
		9	**VINAY**
		13	**TULLINS**
74	***Porte de Chartreuse	13	**VOIRON** Chartreuse liqueur comes from here and you can visit the distillery. Voiron is a manufacturing town.
	N.520	15	**ST. LAURENT-DU-PONT**
		6	**LES ECHELLES**
	N.6	22	*Savoie* **CHAMBÉRY (Connect Route 12)**
	N.491 ***du Sierroz **La Plage **DU PÊCHEUR	15	**AIX-LES-BAINS** Probably the most beautiful and fashionable spa and health resort in France. There is a statue of Queen Victoria as a reminder of the time she spent here. The curative properties of the sulphur springs were known to the Romans. With the Palace of Savoy, beautiful gardens, casinos, shops, Aix-les-Bains is deserving of its popularity. Town Hall, 16thC château; Roman arch and temple; Museum of Archaeology; Fauré Museum: Corot, Degas, Cézanne, Pissarro, Rodin.

MICHELIN MAP NO.	ROAD NO. CARAVAN SITES	Km.	
	N.201	12	**ALBENS**
		3	**ST. FELIX**
77	****Le Belvédère**	18	*Haute-Savoie* **ANNECY**

ANNECY
Capital of the département, an old town with an impressive 12thC castle and streets of arcades, Annecy is principally industrial. It is situated most beautifully on Lake Annecy. There are boat trips on the lake and an aerial railway at Veyrier. At the lake is an indicator by which the various mountain peaks can be identified. St. Maurice, 15thC; St. Pierre Cath., 16thC. Museum: local history.

		18	**CRUSEILLES**
74		16	**ST. JULIEN-EN-GENEVOIS**
70		9	**GENEVA** (Switzerland) **(Connect Route 18)**